THE PSYCHOLOGY OF TERRORISM

What is terrorism? Can anyone be radicalized? How can we respond to terrorist acts?

The Psychology of Terrorism seeks to explain why some acts of violence are considered terrorism and others are not, and why some individuals may be more susceptible to engaging in radical terrorist behavior. Debunking myths and lazy stereotypes, the book delves into some of the most shocking atrocities of our times to discuss the complex and varied psychological characteristics of individual terrorists, organized groups, and their acts.

While there is no simple solution, The Psychology of Terrorism shows us that a growing reverse radicalization movement and modern interventionist techniques can give us hope for the future.

Neil Shortland is Director of the Center for Terrorism and Security Studies, University of Massachusetts Lowell, USA. His research focuses on the psychological aspects of domestic and international security.

T0087607

THE PSYCHOLOGY OF EVERYTHING

People are fascinated by psychology, and what makes humans tick. Why do we think and behave the way we do? We've all met armchair psychologists claiming to have the answers, and people that ask if psychologists can tell what they're thinking. The Psychology of Everything is a series of books which debunk the popular myths and pseudo-science surrounding some of life's biggest questions.

The series explores the hidden psychological factors that drive us, from our subconscious desires and aversions, to our natural social instincts. Absorbing, informative, and always intriguing, each book is written by an expert in the field, examining how research-based knowledge compares with popular wisdom, and showing how psychology can truly enrich our understanding of modern life.

Applying a psychological lens to an array of topics and contemporary concerns – from sex, to fashion, to conspiracy theories – The Psychology of Everything will make you look at everything in a new way.

Titles in the series:

For further information about this series please visit www.routledgetextbooks.com/textbooks/thepsychologyofeverything/

THE PSYCHOLOGY OF TERRORISM

NEIL SHORTLAND

Routledge
Taylor & Francis Group

LONDON AND NEW YORK

First published 2021
by Routledge
2 Park Square, Milton Park, Abingdon, Oxon OX14 4RN

and by Routledge
52 Vanderbilt Avenue, New York, NY 10017

Routledge is an imprint of the Taylor & Francis Group, an informa business

British Library Cataloguing-in-Publication Data
A catalogue record for this book is available from the British Library

Library of Congress Cataloging-in-Publication Data
A catalog record for this book has been requested

ISBN: 978-0-367-35335-3 (hbk)
ISBN: 978-0-367-35331-5 (pbk)
ISBN: 978-0-429-33074-2 (ebk)

Typeset in Joanna
by Apex CoVantage, LLC
Printed and bound by CPI Group (UK) Ltd, Croydon, CR0 4YY

CONTENTS

ACKNOWLEDGMENTS

It is hard to write a book called The Psychology of Terrorism without referencing the O.G. Psychology of Terrorism scholar, Professor John Horgan, who has spent his career humanizing the perception of "the terrorist" and fighting to bridge the gap between the traditional study of psychology and the study of terrorist offenders. I have been lucky that my thinking on the subject has been heavily influenced by my early years studying under Horgan and many of his closest collaborators: Paul Gill, John Morrison, Emily Corner, Kurt Braddock, and Mary-Beth Altier. If it seems my citations of these individuals are over-eager throughout this book, it is likely the result of an unconscious bias stemming from the years I have spent admiring their work.

I would also like to thank all of the students at the University of Massachusetts Lowell and especially those at the Center for Terrorism and Security Studies with whom I have worked, taught, supervised, or even had a passing conversation. It is in trying to teach them the psychology of the world that I am able to crystalize these thoughts in my own mind. Working with them has also been formative in helping me learn how to explain these concepts as something that is deeply human and an extension of processes and experiences that we all share. Many of the analogies and cases presented throughout this book result from my trying to find the best ways to share and inspire the students who I seek to educate every day.

In addition, I would not be able to write anything of worth without my writing support group who keep me fed and focused: Josephine, Sausage, and Ollie.

1

WHAT IS TERRORISM?

"I know it when I see it."

In an article for the *Washington Post* in the aftermath of September 11, 2001, when Islamic terrorists hijacked four planes and flew them into strategic targets in the United States, killing almost 3,000 and injuring 25,000, Michael Kinsley (2001) wrote:

> The most accurate definition of terrorism may be the famous Potter Stewart standard of obscenity: "I know it when I see it."

The phrase "I know it when I see it" is a colloquial expression often used when we are trying to categorize an observable fact or event, even though the category itself is subjective and lacks clear defining parameters. It stems from a 1964 Supreme Court case (*Jacobellis vs. Ohio*) in which US Supreme Court Justice Potter Stewart described his threshold test for obscenity as "I know it when I see it." Terrorism is often a target for this test in that despite defying a formal (or at least a universal) definition, terrorism often holds a psychological sense of power in which we feel like we know it when we see it.

DEFINING TERRORISM WHEN WE SEE IT

The problem, however, is that while in many cases it is easy to know that an act of terrorism is indeed *terroristic*,[1] there are an increasing number of cases that are "on the fringe." Cases like 9/11, the Boston Marathon bombings (the use of two homemade explosive devices, left at the finish line of the Boston Marathon in 2013), and the 7/7 bombings in London (in which four individuals detonated suicide explosive devices across London) are clear, and in a definitional sense, easy. But what about those cases that are not so self-evident and indeed require a sense of psychological interpretation? In these instances, not only is it *harder* for us to know if an act is terrorism or not (not helped by the fact that the experts themselves can often disagree), but in the absence of formal guidelines, we often allow the media or public consciousness to define what *is* and *is not* terrorism. This is problematic because we know from the study of decision-making that people often develop and apply schemas (mental models that help us interpret events) that are driven by ideas about what a prototypical "terrorist attack" or even a "terrorist" *should* look like.

Before we go into the outline of what terrorism is, from a definitional and psychological sense, perhaps it would be good for readers to test what they *think* terrorism is, and most importantly, why. Next I will outline six cases. Some involve terrorism, and some do not. While I ask you to consider this question from a psychological standpoint (what do you *think* is an act of terrorism), you can also think about this from a legal standpoint (what would result in a criminal *conviction* for an act of terrorism). We will start with an easy case, a warmup if you will, and then add in a few new elements of complexity.

CASE 1

In 2014 a hatchet-wielding man, Zale H. Thompson, attacked four New York City Police Department (NYPD) officers on a crowded sidewalk in Queens. He was obsessed with the Islamic State of Iraq and Syria (ISIS) and was known to have spent hours online engrossed in terrorist material. Zale converted to Islam in 2012 and reportedly self-radicalized on the Internet. The police reported that his Internet search history within the nine months preceding the attack included 277 websites related to beheadings, al-Qaeda, ISIS, and al-Shabaab. Thompson's parents described him to CNN as a "depressed recluse."

CASE 2

In 2013 in the United Kingdom, two individuals attacked Fusilier Lee Rigby, a British soldier, near his barracks in Woolwich, southeast London, England. Michael Adebowale and Michael Adebolajo ran Lee Rigby down with their car before using knives to hack him to death in broad daylight. After the attack (while the attackers waited for the police), a cell phone video was recorded in which the two men declared their violent extremist ideology. They had nonworking guns and waited for the police to arrive at the scene, at which time they charged at the police and were nonfatally shot. In the sentencing the judge presiding over the trial commented (from *The Guardian*, 2014):

> It is no exaggeration to say that what the two of you did resulted in a blood bath. Aspects of all this were seen, as they were intended to be, by members of the public. Once you had finished, and again in order to achieve maximum effect, you then carried and dragged Lee Rigby's body into the road in Artillery Place and dumped it there – thus eventually bringing the traffic to a halt.
>
> In the thirteen minutes that passed between then and the arrival of the armed officers, the number of members of the public at the scene grew. You both gloried in what you had done. Each of you had the gun at one point or another and it was used to warn off any male member of the public who looked as though he might intervene.

CASE 3

Between March 2 and 22, 2018, five package bombs exploded in and around Austin, Texas, killing two people and injuring another five. The suspect was 23-year-old Mark Anthony Conditt of Pflugerville,

Texas, who blew himself up inside his vehicle after he was pulled over by police on March 21. The attacks were described as "19 days of terror"[2] and hundreds of law-enforcement officers worked around the clock to track down the attacker. Conditt was an unemployed college dropout. In a 2012 blog for a government class he was taking, Conditt identified himself as politically conservative and argued against abortion and gay marriage. In a final audio recording he made, he described himself as a "psychopath" and said he feels as though he has been disturbed since childhood and that he wishes he were sorry but is not. His recoding offered no explanation for his actions nor how he chose his victims, but he acknowledged that his actions would leave family members without loved ones and would cause permanent injury to others.

CASE 4

On October 1, 2017, Stephen Paddock opened fire from his hotel window into a crowd of approximately 22,000 concertgoers attending a country music festival on the Las Vegas Strip. Paddock fired on the crowd for ten minutes before stopping. He then killed himself in his hotel room. After an extensive review of the case, police reported that there was "no clear motive." Paddock's brother (cited in Lemieux, 2018) was reported to have

> believed Paddock may have conducted the attack because he had done everything in the world he wanted to do and was bored with everything. If so, Paddock would have planned the attack to kill a large amount of people because he would want to be known as having the largest casualty count. Paddock always wanted to be the best and known to everyone.

Another of his brothers told investigators that "Paddock was suffering from mental illness and was paranoid and delusional." A Las Vegas doctor, identified as Paddock's primary care physician, told investigators he believed that Paddock may have had bipolar disorder, but he had refused medication to treat it. He also described Paddock's behavior as "odd." Paddock's attack was the deadliest mass shooting in America, killing 58 and injuring over 800. The previous most deadly attack was the Pulse nightclub shooting in Orlando on June 12, 2016, in which Omar Mateen killed 49 civilians. In his 911 call during the attack, he referred to the Boston Marathon bombers as his "homeboys" and told the negotiators he was a soldier of ISIS.

CASE 5

Jac Holmes was a British volunteer with the Kurdish YPG (People's Protection Units) militia who fought against ISIL in Syria from January 2015. The YPG is a Kurdish group working in Syria, and Turkish leaders view the YPG as a terrorist organization. The YPG is viewed as an extension of the Kurdistan Workers' Party (PKK), which has fought for Kurdish autonomy in Turkey. In 2019 the US Department of State maintained the Foreign Terrorist Organization (FTO) designation of the PKK, pursuant to Section 219 of the Immigration and Nationality Act (INA), as amended (8 U.S.C. § 1189). The PKK was originally designated as an FTO in 1997. Jac documented his time with the YPG on Facebook, as well as on Instagram, and he even did a few Reddit AMAs ("Ask Me Anything," about his time in Syria). His Instagram page shows some of his daily activities, including engaging in sniper battles and attacking ISIS-held villages. The post was accompanied by the quote "223 YPG Sniper Team. We have been operating in raqqa for the past 2 months. We've been shot to shit, set on fire, surrounded. But we still out here @ypgsniper." Facebook videos he posted include him showing off the dead bodies of ISIS fighters who had died during a firefight he had just been in. In the two years Jac fought for the YPG, he returned to the UK and gave lectures abroad about the fight against ISIS. He was due to return home in November 2017, but he died in Raqqa on October 23, 2017, while clearing mines from the city. A national news headline read "BRIT HERO TRAGEDY: Brit volunteer fighter Jac Holmes killed by landmine in Syria just days after booting ISIS fanatics out of terror capital Raqqa."[3]

CASE 6

Jack Letts was a British Canadian national who converted to Islam and fled his home in Oxford, England, in 2014 to join the terrorist organization ISIS in its self-declared capital, Raqqa. He is believed to have married an ISIS bride in Iraq and was given the nickname "Jihadi Jack" by British media. In a 2016 interview Letts stated, "I'm not ISIS, but I believe in the Sharia; I also think that whatever I say, the media will probably freestyle with it and make up more nicknames for me" (Shebab, 2016). When questioned about the treatment of Muslims in Syria, he said, "The Muslims in Syria are burned alive, raped, abused, imprisoned and much more. I also think that some of Muslims I met here are living like walking mountains. Full of honour." When asked if he was a terrorist, he stated: "Do you mean by the English government's definition, that anyone that opposes a non-Islamic system and man-made laws? Then, of course, by that definition, I suppose they'd say I'm a terrorist, khalas ('and that's that')." He also said, "that doesn't mean I am with you, the dirty non-Muslims." Now, Jack Letts is not the subject of this case (he has had his citizenship stripped by the UK government for his involvement in ISIS). In March 2015, after learning that Jack's parents (John Letts and Sally Lane) had sent £223 (roughly $300) to Jack after he had given his word that the money would have "nothing to do with jihad," the police seized their computers and devices, and the couple were formally warned that they could be prosecuted for sending their son property or money. The conversation, as cited in Dearden (2019), went as follows: After learning of the raid on his parents' home, Jack responded, "Please convey to the British police that I'm not planning on coming back to their broken country . . . convey to them from me 'die in your rage soon you'll be the ones being raided!'" Police later provided a second warning that "sending money to Jack is the same as sending money to ISIS." However, in December 2015 Jack indicated that he would like to leave Syria, and his father told their family liaison officer that Jack was "desperate to get out" and "in danger." Lane told her son, "We know you are in danger, so we feel we have no choice but to help you and send it." She attempted two more money transfers which were blocked, and the defendants were arrested. Judge Nicholas Hilliard QC, who was presiding over the case, said, "It was one thing for parents to be optimistic about their children and I do acknowledge he is your son who you love very much. But in this context, you did lose sight of realities."

KNOWING IT WHEN WE SEE IT?

There are several different lenses that we may use to decide if something is an act of terrorism or not. Let's go with the first "lens," the idea that terrorism terrorizes. In this sense, those acts that cause the most fear and uncertainty, or that scare a population, are acts of terrorism. This is often a natural reaction, and many events that cause terror are instinctively called terrorism. So with this "emotion-based" approach, there are a few cases presented in this chapter that involve the public being terrorized. Cases 3 and 4 specifically involved mass instances of harm in that the incidents targeted the general population with no clear targeting strategy and a mass-casualty approach in which a large portion of the population was now at risk of becoming a victim. Cases 1 and 2 are more borderline in this instance. These attacks did terrorize, but they were targeted against a more focused group/individual. In Case 1 officers of the NYPD were the target, and in Case 2 Fusilier Lee Rigby was targeted as a representative of the armed forces. In both instances, civilian targets were actively avoided despite the opportunity in both cases to target them. Thus, despite being most in tune with the emotional reaction to acts of mass casualty violence, an emotion-based approach is not ideal for defining terrorism because of a tendency to call all acts that cause mass harm or fear terrorism. This is a reaction we often see in the public consciousness after an act that causes large-scale casualties. A good example of this would be when ex-police officer Christopher Dorner committed a series of shootings against police officers, their families, and civilians. He was referred to by the Los Angeles

Police Department (LAPD) as a "domestic Terrorist,"[4] and his acts were described as "an act, and make no mistake about it, of domestic terrorism. This is a man who has targeted those who we entrust to protect the public. His actions cannot go unanswered." Now, definitionally, no scholar would define it as such, but this links into the feeling of being terrorized. Thus, despite involving large-scale terror and significant harm to civilian lives, often we cannot rely solely on *being terrorized* as a definition of terrorism.

An alternate approach may be a "tactic-based" approach. This view would also favor Cases 3 and 4 in which the individual used weapons that are associated with acts of terrorism. Explosive devices are often associated with acts of terrorism, and in the United States, at least, the use of firearms is relatively frequent in acts of terrorism committed by lone individuals. The problem with this approach is that research on the history of terrorism, and indeed its evolution, has found that tactics change. David Rapoport categorized terrorism into "four waves" that have occurred since the 1880s. The first is anarchic terrorist violence (1880–1920), the second is anti-colonial (1920–1960), the third is the emergence of the New Left (1960–2000), and the fourth (and current) is the rise of religiously orientated (1980s onward). Now there are not distinct boundaries between waves, and some are still ongoing as are the debates on this concept of "waves" and their boundaries.[5] What is known about the waves is that different forms of weaponry and attack styles are associated with different types of terrorism. This makes a "tactic-based" approach very hard to enforce because, despite the psychological power of an improvised explosive device, even religious groups who heavily leaned toward improvised explosive devices have had to adapt and adopt new forms of weaponry. Furthermore, when we look at the certain enduring groups who have been associated with the use of explosives (such as the Provisional Irish Republican Army or al-Qaeda), despite an early attachment to a certain form of weaponry, in an effort to endure, such groups have had to adopt new organizational structures and new recruiting practices and in doing so adopt to employ smaller scale, cruder methods of attack. This is why in the United Kingdom, for example (where access to firearms is much lower), we see the use of knives (Case 2), as well as the use of vehicles as a weapon (where the individual drives into large crowds). We have also seen vehicle attacks in the United States and France. Also, with reference to the use of firearms, in the United States this method, while deadly, is also often used by mass shooters who are not terrorists. Thus, despite terrorizing *and* using weapons that are often deployed in terrorist attacks, we cannot rely solely on the method of the attack.

One alternate approach is to focus on a "legal-based" definition of terrorism, in which we can judge an act as *terroristic* based on whether the individual was sentenced for a crime that is established as a terrorist-related offense. Such approaches are a good way of consistently deciding what is and what is not terrorism, and academics, for example, often use this approach to decide who to include and not to include in research on terrorist offenders. The issue, however, is that the decision on what is and what is not terrorism would now be based on interpretations of written law (which often have to be amended after acts of terrorism). For example, Dylann Roof (see Chapter 6) was not convicted of terrorist offenses despite being viewed as a white supremacist, posing with symbols of white supremacy, and writing a manifesto in which he outlined his extremist views. GQ magazine even referred to him as "A Most American Terrorist." The issue in this case, and many others that do not reach the legal threshold for terrorism, is that federal law defines domestic terrorism as violent acts occurring within the United States "intended to intimidate or coerce a civilian population." Hence, legal definitions include an additional hurdle of "intimidation" and coercion. In legal terms, because the Boston Marathon bombers used bombs, they could be charged with "using a weapon of mass destruction," which is a crime specified in the US criminal code section for terrorism. Attorney General Loretta Lynch, on the other hand, argued that Roof's manifesto and views (such as his "discriminatory views towards African Americans" and his decision to target "parishioners at worship") made this a clear-cut hate crime.

The legal approach therefore results in somewhat surprising conclusions. For example, the legal definition would define Case

6 as terrorism, yet cases like Dylann Roof's would not be. This in fact reflects the wider trend in the use of terrorism legislation. In a review of terrorism-related charges by New York University's Center for Law and Security, in 2011, 87.5% of terrorism prosecutions were for material support (a sharp rise from 11.6% as recently as 2007; Terrorist Trial Report Card, 2011). Thus, from a legal standpoint, despite John Letts and Sandy Lane not intimidating or coercing, because their actions were linked to a formal terrorist organization, the act of passing finances to their son could legally be charged as a terrorist-related offense.

To put this point in perspective, in a project I conducted with Professor John Horgan, we used the definition of a conviction for a terrorist-related offense to determine who we would define as a member of al-Qaeda. Here, alongside terrorist attackers, our definition included parents and friends who helped hide information, or people who (sometimes unknowingly) provided funding to a terrorist group. Thus, this may be why many may find a legal definition unsatisfactory because what is defined as terrorism is based on what can be argued in court. In this sense it is the antithesis of the emotion-based approach.

One final approach is a "psychological-based" approach in which we need to have a sincere understanding of the psychology of the offender and what they truly hope to achieve in their act of terrorism. Assaf Moghaddam defines terrorism as a "politically motivated violence, perpetrated by individuals, groups, or state-sponsored agents, intended to instill feelings of terror and helplessness in a population in order to influence decision making and change behavior" (Moghaddam, 2005, p. 161). We can debate the "violent" part of this definition later in the book, but for now let us focus on the key psychological term, *motivation*, and the key outcome, *to influence decision making and change behavior*. So, from a psychological sense, terrorism is an act that has a political motivation and is designed to seek political change (or a change in current political influence). Now a psychological approach is interesting, because we no longer define the act by the actions (i.e., tactics) or indeed the degree of harm caused (i.e., the degree of terror), but instead the definition is based on the question of, if at the time of the offense, in the individual's own mind, was he/she acting with the purpose of achieving a political change? In Case 2 we see this in the video recording of Michael Adebolajo taken at the scene; still clutching his weapons and his hands covered in blood, he said:

> The only reason we've killed this man today is because Muslims are dying daily by British soldier. . . . This British soldier is one – he is an eye for an eye and a tooth for a tooth. . . . We must fight them. I apologise that women had to witness this today. But in our land our women have to see the same. You people will never be safe. Remove your government, they don't care about you. You think David Cameron is going to get caught in the street when we start bussin' our guns? You think politicians are going to die? No it's going to be the average guy, like you, and your children. So, get rid of them. Tell them to bring our troops back so you can all live in peace.[6]

In this instance, the motivation is clear: to cause a political change in the way the governments are operating in the Middle East. Now we have the clear question of "but was it going to have an effect?" (i.e., did this attack have a high chance of political effect?). The answer is clearly no. The United Kingdom government is unlikely to remove all of its troops from Afghanistan and Iraq, but in the mind of the perpetrator, this was their motivation. It is this sense, and this subtle bridge between action, motivation, and intention, that is often at the heart of the definition debate. For example, in Cases 2 and 3, there is no clear political ideology driving motivation, and thus despite the significant and awful harm and terror caused, we cannot declare the perpetrator a terrorist. Now this does not minimize what they did or their act; it simply speaks to the fact that of the many motivations driving these individuals' actions, there was no attempt (that we know of) to seek political change.

This is the problem with a psychologically-based approach: we require "overt indicators" of intent based on either (1) their behavior or (2) their narratives and/or expression of ideology. Now, while it is well known that before engaging in terrorist actions, individuals often do express their grievances (and sometimes their intentions, Silver et al., 2018),[7] in some cases they do not, in which case we have to infer motivations and decide if their actions were or were not in support of a political goal. And while the searches for motive often occur (there were extensive attempts to understand the motivations of Mark Anthony Conditt and Stephen Paddock), if they do not turn up a clear political motive, we cannot define the acts as terrorism.

This approach gets more complicated still when we have to differentiate between a crime committed because of a hatred of a certain racial or religious population and a crime committed with hopes of creating a change in the political treatment of these groups. This creates an incredibly fine line between a hate crime (in which you target someone because of the group they represent) and an act of terrorism. One interesting example of this is the case of Elliot Rodger, who is part of a recent trend of mass shooters referred to as involuntary celibates (Incels), an online subculture that defines themselves via their inability to find a sexual partner. Their motivations are often driven by resentment, misogyny, self-loathing, and a sense of entitlement to sex. They also endorse violence against "Stacys" (females who are unattainable to them) and "Chads" (men who they view as muscular and popular). Incels have to date committed at least four mass shooting events that have resulted in the deaths of 45 individuals. Now while Incels are not usually thought of as terrorist offenders, there are cases in which the individuals' motivation and hatred of "Chads" and "Stacys" moves into politic views of how the government should behave. Consider, for example, this extract from Elliot Rodger's (2014) manifesto:

> In order to completely abolish sex, women themselves would have to be abolished. All women must be quarantined like the plague they are, so that they can be used in a manner that actually benefits a civilized society. In order carry this out, there must exist a new and powerful type of government, under the control of one divine ruler, such as myself. The ruler that establishes

this new order would have complete control over every aspect of society, in order to direct it towards a good and pure place. At the disposal of this government, there needs to be a highly trained army of fanatically loyal troops, in order to enforce such revolutionary laws.

The first strike against women will be to quarantine all of them in concentration camps. At these camps, the vast majority of the female population will be deliberately starved to death. That would be an efficient and fitting way to kill them all off. I would take great pleasure and satisfaction in condemning every single woman on earth to starve to death. I would have an enormous tower built just for myself, where I can oversee the entire concentration camp and gleefully watch them all die. If I can't have them, no one will, I'd imagine thinking to myself as I oversee this. Women represent everything that is unfair with this world, and in order to make the world a fair place, they must all be eradicated.

A few women would be spared, however, for the sake of reproduction. These women would be kept and bred in secret labs. There, they will be artificially inseminated with sperm samples in order to produce offspring. Their depraved nature will slowly be bred out of them in time.

To many this would read as a political intent; indeed, if the subject of the manifesto was changed to a religious subgroup, then this would be a clear instance of terrorism based on the espoused ideology within the manifesto.

This all leaves the interesting case of Case 5 – Jac Holmes. Now, from a tactics-based approach, like Jack Letts, Jac Holmes left the United Kingdom to join an offshoot of a formal terrorist group, operating in a civil war against a formal terrorist organization (ISIS). Holmes had no prior military training; he became a sniper with the YPG and was one of the longest-serving foreign volunteers in the fight against ISIS. So from a tactics-based approach he may appear to be a terrorist. He was engaged in a guerrilla war between two fighting insurgent groups within a civil war. He was a sniper, and thus we can assume he killed members of ISIS. From a legal standpoint, while there is a debate around the legality of his actions, other fighters who have joined the YPG have been arrested on return, and under the British law, areas such as Northern Syria are designated as no-go areas, meaning that by even being in that region, Holmes could have been convicted of terrorist-related offenses. Now, if we adopt a psychological-based approach and look at Holmes's motivations, did he have the *motivation to influence decision making and change behavior*. But on an emotional-based approach, many would argue that Holmes is not a terrorist and indeed was there for positive reasons and trying to improve a situation, which at that time was in dire need of support. His mother, Angie Blannin, said the 24-year-old was a "hero in my eyes," and at his funeral hundreds of members of the British Kurdish community and anti-ISIS fighters attended the small Dorset community hall.[8] Thus while Holmes may satisfy all major criteria for a definition, we still may not be comfortable defining him as a terrorist given that while his actions may have been terroristic, he was doing it against a greater terrorist threat. This case then gets even more complicated when we think about how people from different regions (such as those who have previously suffered from YPG terrorist attacks) may evaluate Jac Holmes.

CONCLUSIONS: KNOWING IT WHEN WE SEE IT

The reason why terrorism is so hard to define is because of the double-edged psychological sword within which it operates. On one side we have the psychological *reaction* to acts of terrorism. Acts of terrorism terrorize, and this is part of what makes them unique. It is the civilian audience (and governments) who are their actual targets and who terrorist groups and actors seek to influence through their actions. And this has always led terrorist organizations to lean toward, where possible, methods of attack that create the largest psychological reaction: bombings, public spectacles, and mass spectaculars, to name a few. But terrorism is not the only threat in the world that terrorizes (in fact many argue that terrorism is far from the most terrorizing threat we face based on the number of casualties it causes). As I finish this book, we face the global threat of COVID-19 (which just yesterday officially killed more Americans than the 9/11 attacks), but what can happen is that we declare all acts that terrorize us as terroristic. In this sense, we define terrorism by our reaction to it and not the merits of the individual act itself.

Looking at the act itself, we have another psychological hurdle to overcome; we have to understand the psychology and the intention of the individual and the degree to which they felt that their actions (violent or nonviolent) would, in a near or distant future, create a political change in the world. In some cases, this decision can be easy; they joined a terrorist group or shared extremist views and the motivation for their attack online. But in some cases, this decision is not so black and white, and we must instead use the information that we have available to us to decode the degree of their motivations. It is in this space that creates difficulties in defining acts of terrorism because we rely so heavily on understanding (or at least inferring) the motivations of the individual. In some instances, there are no indicators at all of motivation (the cases of Paddock and Conditt); in other instances, while the motivations are known, we find ourselves debating the degree to which the act sought to create a political change.

So how do we define an act of terrorism? I often adopt a simple three-pronged rubric to define an act as terrorism. In involves an actor (the individual doing an act), a victim (the person who directly suffers as a result of the actors' actions), and an intended audience/ target (a wider target, often a government, whose behavior the actor hopes will change). With this rubric, what is most important is the presence of the intended audience/target. It is not perfect (for example, how sure are we that in our case of the attack against the NYPD officers, the individual was trying to influence a wider target?), but it helps us to differentiate between acts that terrorize (Paddock and Conditt) and acts of terrorism (Thompson and Adebowale and Adebolajo).

To use this rubric in your own life, when you encounter or see an act of harm, mass shootings, stabbings, or even bombings, ask yourself the question "who is the intended target of this activity?" If the target is the people who have been harmed, then in many cases this is not terrorism but simply (and sadly) mass casualty violence or a hate crime. If, on the other hand, the person is using their actions with a view to achieving a political goal or change, then you may be able to define the act as an act of terrorism.

2

WHO IS A TERRORIST?

"[The offender] was known to authorities."

The quotation presented here is one that we often hear in the aftermath of a terrorist attack. Michael Adebowale and Michael Adebolajo (outlined in Chapter 1) were known to intelligence agencies prior to murdering Fusilier Lee Rigby.[1] Nidal Malik Hassan, the former US Army major convicted of killing 13 people and injuring more than 30 others in the Fort Hood mass shooting on November 5, 2009, had his emails analyzed by the FBI prior to his attack (Webster et al., 2012). Man Haron Monis, who took hostages in a siege at the Lindt Chocolate Café at Martin Place, was risk assessed the day before he held siege to a Lindt coffee store in Australia.[2] Tamerlan Tsarnaev, the elder brother of the Boston Marathon bombers, was known to the United States authorities, as were the bombers in the 9/11, 7/7, and November 2015 Paris attacks. More recently still, on November 29, 2019, two people were stabbed and died in Central London. The attacker, Usman Khan, had been released from prison in 2018 and was on license for serving a sentence for terrorist offenses.

The fact that we hear this phrase often speaks to one of the most central debates we have had in the psychology of terrorism: understanding who will become a terrorist. It is a crucial debate and one that needs the input of psychologists. But alas, it is not an easy puzzle to solve. From a theoretical standpoint, we argue about what specifically terrorism, and therefore the terrorist actually is. From a practical standpoint, there are so many individuals who experience the kinds of risk factors that we commonly associate with involvement in extremism (stress, isolation, a grievance, exposure to an extremist narrative) that even the best crafted "profile" will struggle to help us narrow the field. But at the same time, given the significant human, psychological, and economic cost of even the smallest, single-actor terrorist attack, psychologists need to help understand the pathway toward terrorism so we can help identify and, most importantly, prevent individuals from engaging in terrorist activity.

Psychologists (as well as criminologists and political scientists) have debated who is a terrorist since the earliest conversations about terrorism and psychology. For example, in his seminal 1991 text The Fanatics, Max Taylor (one of the first psychologists to study terrorism from a psychological standpoint) sought to explain political violence through a behavioral lens, and even in this early work Taylor (1991, p. 13) noted some prevailing trends that persist even through to today. For example, he highlights how

> when we attempt to account for other people's actions, it has been shown that we tend to show distinctive biases in the kinds of explanations we chose that are not wholly based on objective evidence. In particular, we have a strong tendency to overemphasize dispositional features of people at the expense of situational and environmental causes. "He is that kind of person" (with its implied reference to personality-like qualities). This process is termed by social psychologists as the fundamental attribution error. Conversely, we tend more readily to attribute the causes of our own behavior to situational causes.

What Taylor is talking about here is the tendency to over-apply the role of the person in comparison to the environment. This is something that psychologists call the "fundamental attribution error." Let's take an example I often use with students. I want you to imagine that you fail a basic test in class. Now, when you reflect on your own failure you will likely identify several issues in the environment that impacted your performance (the teacher was poor, you were tired, the test was confusing, the test "didn't matter much"). However, let us imagine also that one of your friends failed. The fundamental attribution error would mean that when it comes to someone else's behavior, you would be far less sympathetic to their environment in explaining their behavior. In this case we may just assume that they failed because they are stupid. In terrorism we often do the same. We have the tendency to explain their behavior via the *person* and not the environment.

As we will show in this chapter, this overemphasis on factors associated with the *person* rather than their *situation* led to decades of search for the all-elusive "terrorist profile," which despite never being found still permeates both academic and popular media circles today. We will move through the different phases of thinking about *who* becomes a terrorist from a focus on the person to a focus on the environment and toward what we would now view as an interactionalist or integrated model that includes both the person and the environment in which they are placed. This latter lens has allowed the psychology of terrorism to better match the presuppositions of psychology in general in that we are, largely, a result of an interaction between core personality factors (and biological and neurological factors) and the environment to which we are exposed.

THERE AND BACK AGAIN[3]

An intuitive view of terrorism is that because the terrorist attacks are so "extreme" (in that they deviate so much from the norms of behavior), the people who engage in such attacks must also display this characteristic (they too, for example, must have extreme personality traits). Now, historically, this led many psychologists on a quest to identify these extreme personality traits that would be able to differentiate "the terrorist" from "everyone else." Two criminologists in London, Paul Gill and Emily Corner, recently documented this search in a paper that explored the journey psychologists have taken in the study of "terrorist personalities."[4] They outline how one of the earliest assumptions was that terrorists were psychopaths (driven largely by the degree of harm that terrorism causes). In the early 1970s and 1980s, for example, several psychologists argued that terrorists were either sociopaths or psychopaths (both forms of antisocial personality disorder, but psychopaths are traditionally viewed as more manipulative and better able to lead a normal life), or that terrorism, in general, was an outlet for those with underlying mental illnesses. However, a lack of evidence for these views (i.e., researchers found that the rates of psychopathy in terrorist samples were not significantly higher than the general population) led to the demise of this view. They simply could not find a single defining "trait" that separated terrorists from everybody else.

After abandoning the view that psychopathy, sociopathy, or other mental illnesses were the sole "silver bullet" to knowing who would become a terrorist, psychologists instead looked to personality in general as the cause. They began by focusing on personality traits that also happen to be associated with psychopathy and sociopathy, with the most studied being narcissism. Pearlstein (1991), for example, said that narcissism was the most complete and "intellectually satisfying theory regarding the personal logic of political terrorism." In his view, terrorist violence was the result of "narcissistic rage," in which once an individual's grandiose self-delusion is shattered (by reality), they protect their ego by channeling their rage at the individuals who shattered this delusion.[5] However, once again the limited empirical assessments that existed at that time did not confirm an overarching personality type that explained or defined the terrorist.

So in the mid-2000s, where were we? Well, as a field it seems we had done a good job of rejecting psychological markers of the terrorist, but we had yet to really begin to unpack what psychological factors. In fact, the lay view of the field became that "there was no terrorist profile," "terrorists are not mentally ill," and/or "terrorists have no dominant personality type." These are, in totality, correct, but such blanket phraseology in essence blinds us to the complexity of what we are studying. Instead, a closer statement to the truth is not that "no profile exists," but that "no terrorist profile has been found" (from Merari, circa 2006; cited in Horgan, 2008). The former is a statement of fact; the latter relates that we cannot yet answer the question because we have not yet finished searching. Merari later elaborates on this point (Merari, 2010, p. 253):

> By and large, the opinion that terrorists do not have a common psychological profiles rests on the absence of research rather than on direct findings. A scientifically sound conclusion that terrorists have no common personality traits must be based on many comparative studies of terrorists from different countries and functions, using standard psychological tests and clinical interviews. As such studies have not been published, the only scientifically sound conclusion for now is that we do not know whether terrorists share common traits, but we cannot be sure that such traits do not exist.

To put this point in perspective perhaps it would be easier to take a small detour via a movie that people (secretly) love: Mean Girls.[6] In one of the more famous scenes from the movie, our protagonist Cady Heron (Lindsey Lohan) on entering the high school lunchroom for the first time is given a "guide to North Shore" lunch layout, and in a voiceover, Janice Ian (Lizzy Caplan) explains to new student Cady the many different high school groups and their seating plan:

> You got your freshmen, ROTC guys, preps, JV jocks, Asian nerds, cool Asians, varsity jocks, unfriendly Black hotties, girls who eat their feelings, girls who don't eat anything, desperate wannabes, burnouts, sexually active band geeks, the greatest people you will ever meet, and the worst. Beware of The Plastics.

Now, based on the information presented here, think about the typical psychological profile of a high school student. The answer is clearly that there is not one. The reason is that in attempting to answer that overarching question, one has to ignore the natural nuances that exist within the group. What this means is that by aggregating our level of analysis to the level of "high school students," we lose the nuances that exist between different groups within our target audience. Now, of course, while this scene is fictional and indeed has aged horribly, it outlines what we know: there are discrete differences between groups of individuals who attend high school. Now, in the high school example, psychologists have found significant predictors of which "type" of student a person may become. Let us take sports, for example; research by Peter Newcombe and Gregory Boyle (1995) found that individuals who engaged in school sports were more outgoing (extraverted) and less anxious. Furthermore, not only was involvement in sports associated with certain personality predictors, but elite athletes also had distinct psychological profiles. So while we may not be able to "profile" all high school students, we can identify factors associated with certain types of high school students.

Now we can take this concept and apply it to the psychology of crime and indeed the psychology of terrorism. One starting point is what David Canter (2000) called the "hierarchy of criminal differentiation." The notion of a hierarchy of criminal differentiation was introduced by Canter to highlight the need to search for consistencies and variations at many levels of that hierarchy. The major premise for this hierarchy is that there are some psychologically important variations between people who engage in different types of behavior during a crime, or different types of crime, and that these relate to differences in the people who commit them. A sample hierarchy for terrorism is displayed in Figure 2.1.

With this hierarchy we can work our way through the high school analogy used earlier, and at each stage we can propose a different psychological question to answer. First, we can explore the difference between people who go to high school and those who do not. Beyond this, we can explore the difference between those who engage in sports at high school and those who do not. We can go further still and explore the differences between those who play football, hockey, lacrosse, or golf. Finally, within a single sport, we can explore the differences between those within football, for example, who gravitate

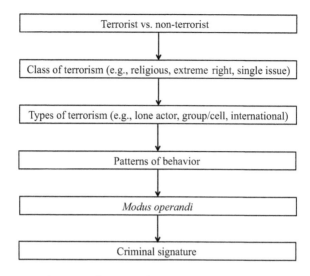

Figure 2.1 A hierarchy for the differentiation of terrorist offenders (from Horgan et al., 2018; adapted from Canter, 2000).

toward quarterback, wide receiver, tight end, and even kicker. When phrased this way, the intuitive psychologist among us probably thinks this makes sense. We know from popular media depictions that different groups of people exhibit different types of personalities, which, to varying degrees, manifest in different types of behavior. It is commonly asserted (in TV shows such as the comedy *Scrubs*, for example) that there are personality differences between pediatricians and surgeons in a hospital. So while we know that there is no "universal" profile, what this hierarchy allows us to do is to try to investigate groups across many different levels of association. The same way it works in sports and hospitals, it can work with terrorist organizations.

DISAGGREGATING BY IDEOLOGY

So what we need to further our understanding of the terrorist is to begin to disaggregate them (separate them into their component parts, and then explore the similarities and differences between these parts). Based on the thinking presented earlier, two things are true: (1) in thinking about the psychology of the *who* becomes a terrorist, we have a clear need to differentiate what we mean by *the terrorist*, and (2) we will find different types of psychological predictors, or differences, between different levels of analysis. In support of these efforts, researchers have begun to identify the differences that exist between individuals who engage in different types of terrorism. Smith (1994) compared individuals who engaged in extreme right-wing terrorism vs. those who engaged in extreme left-wing terrorism in the United States and found that there were significant differences between the two types of offenders in terms of their age, gender, job skills, and education level. Similarly, Handler (1990) found that women were more likely to be involved in extreme left-wing attacks and that left-wing leaders were more likely to be women. Left-wing terrorists were also more educated, whereas right-wing terrorists were much more likely to have a "blue-collar" job. Chermak and Gruenewald (2015) found that women were also more likely to be involved in ecological and animal rights terrorism. Using a dataset of 119 lone-actor terrorists, Gill and his colleagues (2014) also found differences between lone actors who acted in support of a single issue, extreme right or al-Qaeda-related ideology. Depending on the ideology of the offender, there were significant differences in the size of the town in which the individual lived, the amount of university experience they had, their occupation, and their age.

DISAGGREGATING BY GROUP STRUCTURE

An alternate approach has been to investigate whether there are psychological differences between those who engage in terrorism alone vs. as part of a group. While most terrorist individuals are, in some way, affiliated with an overarching group, many groups encourage decentralized leadership and attacks. What this means is that instead of a central "command" authorizing attacks, groups will encourage people to act on their own and without any contact with a formal group. This is referred to as "leaderless resistance" and has been used extensively by a wide range of groups, from anarchists to the Animal Liberation Front to al-Qaeda and ISIS. But this separation of those who operate in a cell (or wider group-based activity) and those who act alone creates an important point of comparison. Paul Gill was one of the very first to explore this and has developed a series of detailed studies that explore not only the behaviors of lone actors (and how they diverge from other forms of actors) but crucially what makes the people who act alone different from those who act as part of a group.

In 2015, Corner and Gill began to compare group and lone-actor terrorists but with a special focus on the role that mental illness may play. As you may remember, mental illness was the first "cause" sought by psychologists but was resoundingly rejected due to the fact that base rates of mental illness were not significantly different between samples of terrorists and non-terrorists. This led to the widely adopted view that terrorists were not mentally ill (and in stating this they usually conflated psychopathy and mental illness in general; Gill & Corner, 2017). The problem, however, was that when viewed at the level of "terrorists" and "non-terrorists," it is true that there is not support for the premise that *all terrorists have a diagnosed mentally illness* or even a specific form of mental illness. But this is not a fair test of the claim.

It was in response to this misinterpreted analysis of mental illness that Corner and Gill began to reexplore the role of mental illness but within a disaggregated frame of analysis. What this means is that instead of adopting the top level of Canter's hierarchy, they moved down a few levels and began to focus on the role of mental illness within lone actors and between lone actors and those who engaged in group-based activities. Their findings were very revealing and indeed formative in the field. Corner and Gill found that lone-actor terrorists were 13.49 times more likely to have a mental illness than a group actor. Lone actors with mental illnesses were more likely to have experienced a recent upcoming life change, to have been a recent victim of prejudice, and/or to have experienced a recent stressor. They also found, in a separate study with the same sample of terrorists, that the prevalence of mental illness decreases between lone mass murderers (those who kill four or more people in a 24-hour span), lone-actor terrorists, solo-actor terrorists (those who conducted an attack alone but were guided by a wider group), lone dyads (two isolated individuals working together), and group-based actors. Corner and Gill also sought to disaggregate what *specific* mental illnesses were prevalent in the sample (going beyond the original focus on psychopathy or sociopathy). They found that, overall, three specific mental illnesses were more prevalent in lone-actor terrorists than both group-based actors and the general population: schizophrenia, autistic spectrum disorder, and delusional disorders.

With these findings in hand, many psychologists, driven by Corner and Gill's work, have now reaccepted the role of mental illness in terrorism, but what has changed is the specificity with which the terrorist and mental illness are discussed. Thus, instead of "terrorists are/are not mentally ill," the truer representation of the fact is that "terrorists who operated alone are more likely than group-based actors and the general population to suffer from schizophrenia, autistic spectrum disorder, or a delusional disorder."

DISAGGREGATING BY BEHAVIOR

In the previous sections we have worked our way down Canter's hierarchy of differentiation. We have seen that there are differences between *who* becomes involved in different types of terrorism, from the far left to the far right. We have also seen that there are differences in those who act alone and those who operate as part of a dyad or group. There is one last lens through which we can look at who becomes a terrorist, which has been employed by psychologists: what *role* they undertake within a terrorist organization. This idea comes from (among a few places) a collaboration that occurred between the International Center for the Study of Terrorism at Pennsylvania State University and their Department of Industrial/Organizational Psychology. Here, researchers began to apply theories and methods from the study of business to the study of the terrorist. The premise here is that al-Qaeda, or the Animal Liberation Front, face the same kinds of issues as Apple, Tesla, or Samsung. This cross-application has since grown, and I/O psychologists (such as Gina Ligon at the University of Nebraska, Omaha, and Matthew Crayne at the University at Albany) have used I/O methods to explore leadership, performance, recruitment, and talent development. One element of I/O psychology is to study the match of the person to the job.[7] The idea here is that certain personality types, or skills, suit certain types of jobs, or roles, better than others. For example, life history theory (LHT) states that individual differences in natural tendencies can be places along a spectrum of slow to fast lifestyles. Fast individuals are more exploitative/antisocial, bold, aggressive, impulsive, and dominant. Slow individuals are more agreeable, conscientious, and honest (Wolf et al., 2007). "Fast" individuals favor immediate benefits rather than long-term strategies to satisfaction, while "slow" individuals favor long-term benefits and can defer the need for immediate gratification. Personality-wise, I am closer to the "fast" end of the continuum, which means I am good at some work-related tasks (innovation, idea generation,[8] taking on new projects) and bad at others (finishing projects, proofreading).[9] We can think about members of a terrorist organization in the same way, not in terms of fast and slow lifestyles specifically but that there is likely to be a matching of person to task within the organization, and, as an extension of this, that different types of personalities are more likely to engage in different types of roles.

TYPOLOGIES OF TERRORIST INVOLVEMENT

Based on the central premise that different types of people engage in different types of behavior within the same organization/group/cell, John Horgan, myself, and a team of research assistants at the University of Massachusetts Lowell sought to explore the possible typologies of terrorist action using the methods that forensic psychologists had used with murderers, sexual offenders, arsonists, and many other varied forms of criminal. Using court reports, media reporting, case studies, and legal documents, we collected data on a sample of 183 individuals who had been convicted of acting in support of al-Qaeda. This included people who had launched attacks in America, those who had joined al-Qaeda and operated in Afghanistan, financiers, and a wide supporting cast of roles. Overall, we collected more than 200 data points per offender (ranging from name, birth place, school education, to how they came in contact with the group, any attack in which they were involved, and what happened to them in court), but what we were really interested in was 45 behaviors that we coded as present or absent for each of these individuals. This collection of behaviors covered the whole spectrum of involvement, from liaising with al-Qaeda via email to detonating explosive devices and everything in between.

To develop typologies, we used a multidimensional scaling method called a smallest space analysis (SSA). SSAs have been used extensively in criminology and forensic psychology to develop typologies of actors, and they are a mathematical way of identifying groups, or themes, of behaviors that are likely to co-occur at the same time. What an SSA does is identify the probability that two variables are likely to co-occur at the same time, and it then presents these likelihoods within a visual two-dimensional space. This visual space is important because it shows all of the behaviors and their relationships with each other in one incorporated space. This allows the viewer to easily see the relationships between variables based on their distance to each other. Our SSA from this paper is shown in Figure 2.2. From this SSA we can glean a few things: we can see that there are some terrorist behaviors that very rarely occur together (behaviors that are not close in the space such as building bombs, "BuildIEDs," top left, and organizing training for potential members, "OrganizeTraining," bottom right).

What we then do, when presented with a blank SSA like the one shown here, is to identify significant distinctions within variables to identify "themes" of action. These themes should represent distinct underlying psychological differences. So, for example, in the SSAs that were developed for instrumental and expressive murders, the distinction represented two fundamentally different underlying motivations

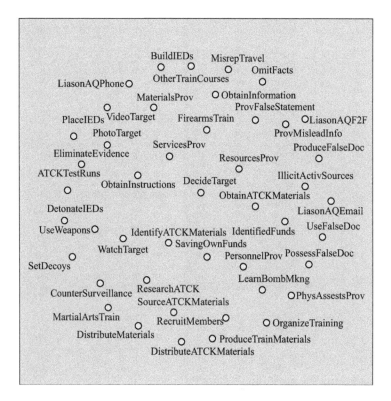

Figure 2.2 SSA of terrorist behaviors (from Horgan et al., 2018).

to commit a murder. Here, our distinctions should show psychologically distinct forms of engagement with a terrorist organization.

There are several ways to cut up an SSA, and that is one of the largest issues with it – that the identification of themes is a subjective process determined by the researcher. Figure 2.3 shows the typology we (the authors) identified. To us, the upper-left section represented behaviors that were involved with launching terrorist attacks. This included building, placing, and detonating improvised explosive devices (BuildIEDs, PlaceIEDs, DetonateIEDs, BombMaking) or using other weapons to launch attacks (UseWeapons). It also included efforts to obtain instructions on how to build explosive devices

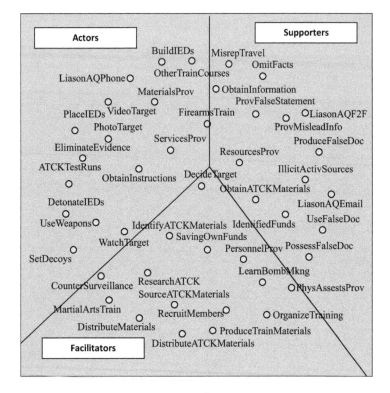

Figure 2.3 SSA with authors analysis of themes.

(ObtainedInstructions). Finally, this theme included behaviors related to attack planning (WatchTarget, PhotoTarget, VideoTarget) and conducting attack test runs (ATCKTestRuns). What these behaviors have in common is that they are directly in support of a violent terrorist attack. We termed this theme "Actors."

The second theme was the top right of the space and represented actions in support of terrorist attacks. These behaviors related to fraudulent and criminal services such as producing, possessing, and using false documents (ProduceFalseDoc, PossessFalseDoc, UseFalseDoc). These individuals also procured funding through illicit means such as the drug trade and running fraudulent charities or businesses (IllicitActivSource). In this we also have behaviors associated with connecting to a wider network such as liaising with members of al-Qaeda via email (LiaseAQEmail) and face-to-face (LiaseAQEmail).

Finally, the lower-middle quadrant of Figure 2.3 represents behaviors that are aimed at generally facilitating the running of a terrorist group. These behaviors include providing resources and services as well identifying, sourcing, researching, and obtaining the materials required to launch an attack (SourceATCKMaterials, IdentifyATCK-Materials, DistributeATCKMaterials, ResearchATCKMaterials). Here we also see recruitment behaviors and organizing training for others (OrganizeTraining).

While the identification of certain themes of behavior is interesting, this alone tells us very little about the *people*. But through a process of theme allocation (in which each individual in the dataset is assigned to a theme 1, 2, 3, or hybrid based on whether their behaviors all reflect one underlying theme), we can examine if there are differences between the type of person who engages in each type of behavior. For example, if an individual engaged in ten behaviors in the Actor theme, five behaviors in the Facilitator theme, and three behaviors in the Supporter theme, they would score 62.5% for the Actor theme (100/16*10), 35.72% for the Facilitator theme (100/14*5), and 20% for the Supporter theme (100/15*3). Because 62.5 > 35.72 + 20, the offender would be assigned to the Actor theme.[10] In our database of 183 terrorist offenders, almost 10% were Actors, 32% were Facilitators, and 15% were Supporters. The remaining sample were hybrids of either theme 2 or 3 types of behavior.

In line with everything we learned from I/O psychology, there were significant differences between the personalities of different types of terrorists in our sample. In terms of their socio-demographics, hybrid offenders ("jack of all trades" if you will) engaged in terrorism younger than those who held supporting positions. Actors were also engaged, overall, for the shortest amount of time compared to the other types of offenders. Facilitators were less likely to be married and have children than the other types of offenders. When we looked at previous convictions, Actors were more likely to have previous convictions for violence, and Actors were also more likely to have converted to Islam (rather than being raised in the religion).

SO WHO DOES BECOME A TERRORIST?

This chapter started with the historical quest for a terrorist profile and the ultimate answer to "who" becomes a terrorist. This question has been a central foundation in the psychological study of terrorism and to this day remains one of the most important questions on which we focus (along with why people become terrorists; see Chapter 3). Overall, if the past few decades have taught us anything, it is that the answer to who becomes a terrorist depends on to whom they are being compared. The simple view that a single personality factor can predict who will and who will not engage in extremist violence has long since been abandoned, but this does not mean that there are not markers. What was missing was specificity. Gill and Corner have been able to show that some factors are very closely related to certain types of action, such as mental health and lone-actor terrorism. The challenge then is to fight the natural urge to make broad generalizations and to view all terrorists as one group but to continue to explore the important nuances that exist between individuals who engage in terrorism, for it may well be true that there is far greater variety between terrorist actors than there is between "terrorists" and "non-terrorists."

3

WHY DO PEOPLE BECOME TERRORISTS?

France's anti-terrorism prosecutors on Saturday took over the investigation of a fatal knife rampage near Paris, saying they had established that the attacker had been radicalized and had carefully planned an act intended to spread terror.

A man identified only as Nathan C. stabbed one person to death on Friday in a park in Villejuif, just outside southern Paris, and wounded two others. The attacker, who had a history of drug and psychiatric problems, was shot dead by police.

"While the troubling psychiatric problems of the individual have indeed been confirmed, the investigations carried out in the last few hours have allowed us to establish a definite radicalization of the suspect, as well as evidence of planning and preparation carried out before the act," the anti-terrorism prosecutor's department said.

(Carraud, 2020)

This statement was reported by Reuters on January 4, 2020. The man in question stabbed one person to death and wounded two others in a suburb of Paris. Just prior to the act he yelled "Allahu Akbar" (Arabic for "God is great"). He was quickly shot and killed by local police. In his backpack, the police found the Quran and other Muslim religious texts. The authorities quickly identified the assailant (identified as

"Nathan C.") and reported that he had a history of psychiatric problems and was a convert to Islam.

Looking at this case, there is a lot here that confirms what we reported in the last chapter. The individual was a lone actor and also had a concurrent mental illness. But at the same time, this statement includes a mercurial new element – that he was "radicalized." Now, it is a safe bet that if you are reading a book about the psychology of terrorism, you have, in some sense, heard the term radicalization. Perhaps you have seen popular media depictions of a "radicalized" individual who seeks to engage in an act of terrorism. Examples abound, and as early as the 1990s, "radicalized" villains proceeded to be a central part of action movies, including everyone's favorite Christmas movie, *Die Hard* (not *Love, Actually*).[1] Consider, for example, *The Rock*. In this movie Alcatraz Island is taken hostage by Marine General Francis Xavier Hummel who for years had protested the government's refusal to pay benefits to families of war veterans who died during secret military operations. The death of his wife, Barbara, on March 9, 1995, drove General Hummel over the edge, and now he decided that the threat of using VX gas warheads and launching them into San Francisco was the only way to get his demands met.[2] The overarching plot is the same as many such action movies in which an individual feeling deeply passionate about a just cause comes to the point in which an act of violence is required to achieve an ultimate goal. The "radicalized Islamist" was a protagonist in Western action movies such as *True Lies* (1994), *Executive Decision* (1996), and *The Siege* (1999), and this has continued with modern shows like *Homeland*, *24*, *Quantico*, *Lie to Me*, and *Criminal Minds*, as well as films like Marvel's *Iron Man* and even the new *Aladdin*, which included a radicalized Islamic terrorist character. While it is out of the scope of this book to comment on the damaging effects of employing the stereotypical "Islamic terrorist" as the de facto villain in media (in terms of creating negative implicit biases and stereotypes),[3] the wider point here is that what is often depicted is a *radicalized* individual who comes to a point where they are willing to engage in acts of harm against an innocent population in order to achieve their goal.

Radicalization is the psychological process of becoming willing to engage in harmful and illegal acts in support of a person's wider ideological belief, and in various guises, and psychologists have identified this process as the solution to *why* somebody becomes involved in terrorism. Radicalization, as we will see, is a complicated process, and there are many who argue about both the nature, role, and even existence of this phenomenon (a personal favorite article is the 2013 *Rolling Stone* piece "Everything You've Been Told About Radicalization Is Wrong," Knefel, 2013). Even today there are those who argue that the individual psychological process is not as important as the wider political landscape. For example, in an article published as I write this book (January 2020), a scholarly expert in the field was quoted as saying (in Hussain, 2020),

> The discourse on jihadism has a misguided focus on individuals, particularly the idea that a meaningful understanding of political violence can be found by getting inside their heads. . . . If you took a random sample of the motivations of U.S. military service members, you would probably find that some believed in their mission, some just needed a job, and some were sadists who wanted to kill people. But you couldn't go directly from analyzing the mindsets of individual soldiers to understanding the political goals or causes of the U.S. wars in Iraq and Afghanistan.

Well, as a psychologist I disagree; the fact that soldiers are not all there for *the mission* tells us something very important about radicalization and is exactly why we *should* study the individual (spoiler alert: many terrorists are also not there for *the mission*). But the wider point here is that while the political purpose is, of course, key, we as psychologists need to understand the psychological process that occurs as someone goes from not wanting to engage in violence to the point at which they have been able to justify the decision to engage in violent (or nonviolent) extremist acts. It is only by better understanding this process that we can seek to prevent it and (as we will see in the next chapter) reverse it.

The goals of this chapter are clear: to articulate what radicalization is, and crucially, what it is not; to outline how psychologists have begun, and continued to, theorize about the radicalization process; and, finally, to outline a case of real-world radicalization so that you, the reader, can begin to understand the immense complexity that exists within the radicalization process.

The study of radicalization is immense, expanding, and ever increasing in complexity. Scholars far smarter than I have even begun to look at the neurological roots of radicalized beliefs, sociologists are engaging in interviews with people who have directly experienced radicalization, and as a field we are identifying an increasing number of factors associated with the process (and even lenses through which to consider the process). Thus, while this chapter cannot be all encompassing, I hope it provides a framework that can be used to consider the many different approaches that are currently being applied to the problem.

WHAT IS RADICALIZATION?

For the purpose of simplicity, we can adopt the descriptive definition of radicalization proposed by Clark McCauley and Sophia Moskalenko (2008) that radicalization means changes in beliefs, feelings, and behaviors in directions that increasingly justify intergroup violence and demand sacrifice in defense of the in-group.

Before we outline the progress made by psychologists in the study of radicalization, we must address a problem: how we do we study this problem? When it comes to radicalization, we are interested in the workings of the mind that are driving behavior, the individual's cognitions, beliefs, values, and critically, how these change over time. This becomes more complicated when we also factor in the idea that certain external factors *cause* these changes. In traditional psychology, measuring an individual's cognitive state is relatively easy. The problem, however, is that traditional psychological methods (e.g., laboratory studies) are slightly harder with terrorist offenders. In the absence of traditional psychological experiments to measure the processes involved in radicalization, researchers have often relied on using established psychological principles to propose theoretical models (often framed as physical metaphors or analogies) to explain the process through which someone becomes radicalized.

One of the first theories of radicalization was the *Pathway to Radicalization*[4] identified by Randy Borum (2003). In a Federal Bureau of Investigation bulletin, Borum outlined a psychological pathway along which an individual develops an ideology that justifies the use of violence. This pathway begins with the view that something *isn't right* (i.e., there is an injustice in the world); this then progresses to the view that this injustice *isn't fair*. In this stage, the current state of affairs is compared to the state of affairs of others, and the individual views this difference as unjust. In psychological terms, you could also argue that they have begun to develop in- and out-group boundaries in which the individual perceives that their in-group is suffering unjustly compared to the out-group. The next stage of this model is to attribute *blame to the other group*. So not only does the individual believe that they are experiencing an injustice in comparison to the out-group but that this injustice is directly the *fault* of the out-group. This now makes the out-group the target and responsible for the aversive experiences of the individual. This leads to dehumanization of the out-group, the development of negative stereotypes toward them, and violence is eventually legitimized because of the immense negative sentiment directed toward the members of the out-group and the view that they are directly responsible for the individual's (or individuals from their in-group's) injustices.

Another popular theory in the field that shares many similarities with Borum's is Moghaddam's Staircase to Terrorism (2005). Moghaddam proposes a six-stair staircase that an individual walks up in order to become radicalized. At the "ground floor," the individual experiences deprivation; they are lacking something that they want/need. People compare the experiences of their group to another and see that they are relatively deprived. This sense of deprivation creates a motivation to improve the group's status. The staircase model now offers an alternate outcome: if the individual has the opportunity to address these injustices through legitimate or political means, they will not continue seeking radical action. However, if they believe that there are no legitimate routes through which they can achieve inter-group balance, they will move up the stairs toward violent action. On the next stair, this discontent is channeled toward a target, and anger is displaced toward them. Similar to Borum's model, there is a strong in-group/out-group boundary line drawn, and negative sentiments and blame are displaced toward the out-group. Among the group of people on this stair are those who begin to believe that radical actions are required. This subset moves to the next stair. Now, on this stair, this small group of radically minded, angry individuals begins to share their grievances and at the same time legitimize and normalize each other's opinions (almost a form of group think,[5] if you will). It is this forming of a very close, very closed group that serves to justify the opinions within that lead to the acceptance of more extreme ideas (such as violence) and allow them to bypass traditional psychological mechanisms that seek to inhibit human actions (such as our aversion to killing). It is at this stage (the fourth stair) where individuals are psychologically "ready" to join a terrorist group. The fifth and sixth stairs in Moghaddam's model involve being assigned a role within a group, and finally, facilitating violence.

What makes these types of theories so appealing is that on the face of it they make intuitive sense. They reflect the narratives that emerge from individuals who engage in terrorist violence and the ideologies of the groups who inspire others to act. Furthermore, from a psychological standpoint, these processes are ideologically diverse, meaning that these models involve universal processes that can occur independent of a specific ideology and meaning that the process that governs someone becoming involved in jihadist violence can be the same as the process that governs someone engaging in far-right, or even far-left, terrorist violence.

We can examine these types of models by looking at the motivations of Anders Breivik. Breivik is a far-right extremist who commit-ted two terrorist attacks in 2011 in Norway. On July 22, 2011, Anders detonated a van bomb in the center of Oslo, killing eight. He then traveled to a Workers' Youth League (AUF) summer camp (a summer camp for politically active youths) on the small island of Utøya, where he proceeded to shoot dead 69 young children. On the day of the attacks Breivik distributed a manifesto titled "2083: A European Declaration of Independence" in which he described his militant ideology, his opposition to Islam, and the "cultural suicide" ongoing in Europe at the time. He also claimed to be a member of the international Christian military order. As his trial began in April 2012, he provided the following opening statement (cited in Seierstad, 2013):

> I stand here today as a representative of the Norwegian and European resistance movement. I speak on behalf of Norwegians who do not want our rights as an indigenous population to be taken away from us. The media and the prosecutors maintain that I carried out the attacks because I am a pathetic, malicious loser, that I have no integrity, am a notorious liar with no morals, am mentally ill and should therefore be forgotten by other cultural conservatives in Europe. They say I have dropped out of working life, that I am narcissistic, antisocial, am prey to bacteria phobia, have had an incestuous relationship with my mother; that I suffer from deprivation of a father, am a child murderer, a baby murderer, despite the fact that I killed no one under fourteen. That I am cowardly, homosexual, pedophile, necrophiliac, Zionist, racist, a psychopath and a Nazi. All these claims have been made. That I am mentally and physically retarded with an IQ of around eighty.
>
> I am not surprised by these characterizations. I expected it. I knew the cultural elite would ridicule me. But this is bordering on farce.
>
> The answer is simple. I have carried out the most sophisticated and spectacular attack in Europe since the Second World War. I and my nationalist brothers and sisters represent all that they fear. They want to scare others off doing the same thing.
>
> Nationalists and cultural conservatives were broken-backed after the fall of the Axis powers. Europe never had a McCarthy, so

the Marxists infiltrated schools and the media. This also brought us feminism, gender quotas, the sexual revolution, a transformed church, deconstruction of social norms and a socialist, egalitarian ideal of society. Norway is suffering from cultural self-contempt as a result of multicultural ideology.

Nationalist and culturally conservative parties are boycotted by the media. Our opinions are seen as inferior, we are second-class citizens and this is not a proper democracy! Look at the Swedish party Sverigedemokraterna and what is happening to them. In Norway, the media have conducted a systematic smear campaign against the Progress Party for twenty years and will go on doing so. Seventy percent of British people see immigration as a major problem and think Great Britain has become a dysfunctional country. Seventy percent are dissatisfied with multiculturalism.

. . . How many people feel the same in Norway, do you think? More and more cultural conservatives are realizing that the democratic struggle achieves nothing. Then it is just a short step to taking up arms. When peaceful revolution is made impossible, then violent revolution is the only option. . . .

People who call me wicked have misunderstood the difference between brutal and wicked. Brutality is not necessarily wicked. Brutality can have good intentions. . . .

If we can force them to change direction by executing seventy people, then that is a contribution to preventing the loss of our ethnic group, our Christianity, our culture. It will also help to prevent a civil war that could result in the death of hundreds of thousands of Norwegians. It is better to commit minor barbarity than major barbarity.

In this speech, we see evidence of the staircase and pathway model. There is a clear feeling of discrimination of his ethnic group, that actions are needed to create equality and protect this group, and that extreme action was required in order to achieve this. At the same time, we can see his views of the out-group, who are viewed as being to blame for the current discrimination he has felt ("Nationalist and culturally conservative parties are boycotted by the media. Our opinions are seen as inferior, we are second-class citizens and this is not a proper democracy"). We also see, as Moghaddam would argue, a perception that democratic means cannot achieve the desired effect ("How many people feel the same in Norway, do you think? More and more cultural conservatives are realizing that the democratic struggle achieves nothing. Then it is just a short step to taking up arms. When peaceful revolution is made impossible, then violent revolution is the only option"). And thus, this constellation of perceived injustices and out-grouping blames attribution and dehumanization results in Breivik undertaking violent terrorist action, which in his view is a necessary step to prevent further discrimination and injustice ("If we can force them to change direction by executing seventy people, then that is a contribution to preventing the loss of our ethnic group, our Christianity, our culture"). Another example would be Dzhokhar Tsarnaev, the younger of the two brothers who undertook the bombing attacks at the Boston Marathon. When surrounded, shot, and facing arrest, he scrawled the following in pencil inside the boat where he was hiding (reported in Bever, 2015):

> The U.S. Government is killing our innocent civilians but most of you already know that. As a M[bullet hole] I can't stand to see such evil go unpunished, we Muslims are one body, you hurt one you hurt us all, well at least that's how Muhammad wanted it to be [bullet hole] ever, the ummah is beginning to rise/awa [bullet hole] has awoken the mujahideen, know you are fighting men who look into the barrel of your gun and see heaven, now how can you compete with that. We are promised victory and we will surely get it. Now I don't like killing innocent people it is forbidden in Islam but due to said [bullet hole] it is allowed. All credit goes to [bullet hole].

Here again we see the same narratives: perceived injustice and the need for violence to prevent further injustice. This is why theories such as the staircase, and pathway, are so convincing and indeed hold such traction in the field; they closely reflect the motivations and justifications that we very often see terrorists giving for their actions.

IS RADICALIZATION THE ANSWER?

The cases presented here show that there is a lot of support for both the existence of radicalization and that the narratives that individuals use to justify their acts often reflect the core components of radical thinking that have been proposed by psychologists. But there is a problem here; we are relying on the narratives that individuals use to justify their own actions, and one of the things that psychologists have often identified is that our description of why we do things is often not the same as the reasons that we do things. Also, by relying solely on their justification, we can find ourselves trapped in a circular logic. Consider this case, when we ask ourselves why individuals engaged in terrorism, the clear answer is often (as shown by the media reporting at the time) that "they were radicalized." But when we look for evidence that they were radicalized, the answer is "that they engaged in terrorism." Thus, engaging in terrorism is both the cause and the evidence for radicalization. This in itself provides a kind of circular logic that we show here:

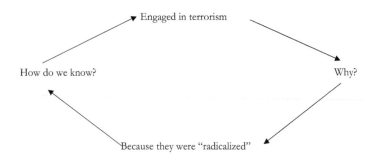

We can see this conceptual model play out in real life. Let us look, for example, at this press release from the U.S. Attorney's Office:

FOUR MEN FOUND GUILTY OF PLOTTING TO BOMB NEW YORK SYNAGOGUE AND JEWISH COMMUNITY CENTER AND TO SHOOT MILITARY PLANES WITH STINGER MISSILES[6]

James Cromitie, aka Abdul Rahman, aka Abdul Rehman; David Williams, aka Daoud, aka DL; Onta Williams, aka Hamza; and Laguerre Payen, aka Amin, aka Almondo, were found guilty today of plotting to detonate explosives near a synagogue and Jewish community center in the Riverdale section of the Bronx, New York, and to shoot military planes located at the New York Air National Guard Base at Stewart Airport in Newburgh, New York, with Stinger surface-to-air guided missiles, announced Preet Bharara, the U.S. Attorney for the Southern District of New York. The four men were arrested on May 20, 2009, in the Bronx after planting what they believed were live explosives at various target locations, and were subsequently indicted on June 2, 2009.

"Homegrown terrorism is a serious threat, and today's convictions affirm our commitment to do everything we can to protect against it," said U.S. Attorney Bharara. "The defendants in this case agreed to plant bombs and use missiles they thought were very real weapons of terrorism. We are safer today as a result of these convictions. We thank the members of the jury for their time and diligent service. We also commend the extraordinary work of the prosecutors, agents, and detectives who demonstrated unyielding dedication during the investigation and prosecution of this case."

According to the complaint, indictment, and the evidence presented at trial before U.S. District Judge Colleen McMahon, in June 2008, an informant working with the FBI was approached by Cromitie in Newburgh. Cromitie explained to the informant that his parents had lived in Afghanistan and that he was upset about the war there. Cromitie expressed interest in returning to Afghanistan and said that if he were to die a martyr, he would go to "paradise." Cromitie also expressed an interest in doing "something to America." The following month, Cromitie and the informant discussed Jaish-e-Mohammed, a Pakistan-based designated foreign terrorist organization, with which the informant claimed to be involved, and Cromitie stated that he would be interested in joining the organization to "do jihad."

THE PLOT[7]

Beginning in June 2008, James Cromitie (who for all intents and purposes is viewed as the ringleader of this cell) began the process of trying to launch a terrorist attack in the United States. His motivations were to retaliate for the United States' current actions abroad, namely the war in Afghanistan which it launched following the 9/11 terrorist attacks. Now, while we will get to how this plot emerged later, the plot that they were convicted for consisted of two planned terrorist attacks: one involved the use of a surface-to-air missile to target and destroy a military aircraft, and the second was to detonate a number of improvised explosive devices at a number of synagogues in the Riverdale section of the Bronx, New York.

Central to this plot (and indeed a source of significant debate ever since) was the role of an FBI informant, Shahed Hussain, who was involved in every step of the plan, from getting the missiles and bombs to running the reconnaissance missions to even teaching the members of the cell the tenets of radical Islam. He also offered financial incentives to carry out the plot.[8] In June 2008 Cromitie approached Hussain and informed him of his issues with the war in Afghanistan. By February 2009, Cromitie and Hussain had conducted some preliminary surveillance on Stewart Airport, and Cromitie had asked Hussain (who at the time was claiming that he was connected to an Islamic terrorist group abroad) whether he could obtain explosives and surface-to-air missiles. Hussain urged Cromitie to recruit others who wanted to join their cell, but Cromitie took no real steps to do so. In fact, by December 2008 Hussain was "exasperated" with Cromitie and asked him to explain "why the first step has not been started. . . . You know, with the target, the recruiting, and the codes."[9] Cromitie's response suggested that he was considering abandoning the plot: "It's not so easy, bro. How you start something like that? I'm trying, then every time I turn around it seems like my, my shit is not, that's not my mission." In February 2009, Cromitie stated that he was no longer going to recruit any other members of the mosque: "I'm not going to involve anyone else" (ibid.). Then followed a six-week period of "radio silence" between Cromitie and Hussain (in spite of persistent efforts by Hussain to initiate contact), and even the FBI concluded that the Cromitie investigation had "gone cold" because he had "backed away from furthering the conspiracy."[10]

Eventually, however, James Cromitie did recruit three other individuals – David Williams, Laguerre Payen, and Onta Williams – and together the four offenders and Hussain discussed possible targets, with the offenders expressing a desire to target military bases and synagogues in the New York area. After they all agreed that the targets were synagogues in the Bronx and a military aircraft at the National Guard base in Newburgh, New York, the offenders began to conduct surveillance on planes that could be targeted, and Cromitie and David Williams traveled with Hussain to Brooklyn, New York, to purchase a semiautomatic handgun for the terrorist operation (*United Sates of America vs. Cromitie et al.*, criminal complaint).

After selecting their targets, Cromitie, David Williams, Payen, and Hussain then drove to a storage locker in Stamford, Connecticut, to collect their surface-to-air missiles and three explosive devices (which they thought had been provided by a foreign terrorist group). On May 20 the FBI arrested the four offenders as they planted their explosive devices at a Jewish center and synagogue in Riverdale.[11]

Cromitie, David Williams, Onta Williams, and Payen were found guilty of attempting to detonate explosives near a Jewish center and a synagogue in the Riverdale section of the Bronx. Cromitie, David Williams, and Onta Williams were each sentenced to 25 years. In a separate sentencing, Payen was also handed a 25-year sentence for his role in the plot.[12]

What is so interesting about this case is that in the days, months, and even years since the arrests were made, two very distinct pictures of the individuals have emerged. The first is that of a radicalized and dangerous terrorist cell. The four foreign-born men were described by federal authorities as "radical Islamists," and the ensuring media reports described Cromitie as "radicalized in a New York prison."[13] Furthermore, looking at the (albeit brief) information presented here, we could arguably see evidence of the core factors of the staircase or pathway model, a sense of injustice about the current war in Afghanistan, and a need to "do something to America." The second view is that these individuals had little radical intent, were victims of an oppressive sting operation, and exhibited few cognitions that would fit our definition of radicalization (e.g., the justification for the use of violence). This case has thus become somewhat of a lightning rod for the discussion of radicalization and the use of sting operations and entrapment. Let us quickly outline the ringleader of this cell and how and why he became involved. Ask yourself, does he seem radicalized to you?

JAMES CROMITIE

James Cromitie was born in Brooklyn, New York, in 1964 to an African American, single-mother home as a middle child of ten. Prior to his involvement in terrorism Cromitie had a record of 27 arrests. Twelve of these arrests were for drug-related offenses. He spent a total of 12 years in state prison before meeting Hussain. Hussain met Cromitie at a mosque he was asked to attend by the FBI to infiltrate the community.[14] After Cromitie met Hussain, they began talking about launching a terrorist attack in America, and Cromitie described that he had long thought about "doing something." He was recorded saying, "if you have the brains and the money, then you can put the team together. . . . The funny thing is, I have the brains. I just don't have the money." (Hussain then responded: "The funny thing is I have the money.") They laughed, and Cromitie said, "two brains is better than one."

In several of his meetings with Hussain, Cromitie reinforced his hatred of Jews and Americans and expressed a desire to kill President Bush. Cromitie even told Hussain that he had wanted to conduct a terrorist attack "since [he] was seven" and that he had considered targeting bridges in New York and even the White House.[15] During the attack planning, he specifically stated that he wanted to lay the bombs at the synagogue:

> I ain't gonna lie, Hak [Hussain]. I think I'd like to do the synagogue thing by myself, Hak. . . .Yeah, I'm serious. I'd like to do that by myself, Hak. [Hussain: What do you think about the military planes?] I don't give a damn who do that. I want to do the synagogue. I have a choice to do what I want, Hak. I'm sorry, brother. I don't care, Hak. That synagogue would fuck a lot of shit up.[16]

But despite his expressions of intent, it is also clear that Cromitie was ill-equipped to achieve any terrorist goals and often seemed hesitant. In fact, the judicial opinion stated that

> There is not the slightest doubt in my [the judge's] mind that James Cromitie could never have dreamed up the scenario in which he actually became involved. And if by some chance Cromitie had imagined such a scenario, he would not have had the slightest idea how to make it happen.[17]

In fact, many viewed Cromitie as more of a fantasist than a fanatic. Cromitie told Hussain that he believed President Bush was the Antichrist, and he wanted to kill him "700 times." He falsely claimed to have visited Afghanistan and to have stolen guns from his job (despite Walmart not selling firearms). He also said he had been jailed for murder and throwing bombs at police stations: all of this was untrue.

In February 2009, Cromitie lied to Hussain that he was in North Carolina and went "radio silent" for six weeks. However, after losing his job (at Walmart), Cromitie reinitiated contact with Hussain, saying that he was "broke and needed to make some money."[18]. He met with Hussain, recommitted to the "mission," and also recruited a new member (David Williams). During the attack planning stages, Hussain offered Cromitie a BMW car, as much as $250,000, a post-attack getaway trip to Miami, Puerto Rico, or Costa Rica, and even a barber-shop of his own if he completed the attack.[19]

Thus, despite being the most committed member and expressing an outward motivation to "do something," it is clear that the personal process of engaging in terrorism in this case was not linear and was influenced by far more mundane factors such as the need for money and material goods. In fact, the role of money (specifically offers of money from Hussain) became a significant part of this case. On May 8, for example, all of the defendants asked Hussain for money to pay bills before the operation.[20] Hussain also admitted at trial that he had offered to buy Cromitie's girlfriend a BMW. Despite this, Hussain frequently confirmed that he did not want recruits who were in it "for the money," and most of them agreed they were not. Although Onta Williams perhaps phrased it best by stating, "I'm doing it for the sake of Allah. I mean, the money, the money helps, but I'm doing it for the sake of Allah."

A TALE OF TWO PYRAMIDS

The goal of the aforementioned case is not to dispel the concept of radicalization. I wholeheartedly believe that radicalization is a very real and very pressing concern, and there are clear cases where an individual undergoes a process in which they have a cognitive shift that leads to the eventual use of violence which they believe will have a significant political effect. What this case shows us, however, is that radicalization alone cannot account for why people become terror-ists. In terms of the psychology of terrorism, we have to expand our scope beyond simply the cognitive shift toward supporting terror-ism, and we must incorporate the behavioral process of becoming involved with and engaging in terrorism. One way to conceptualize this idea, which has gained a lot of traction in the field, is through what Clark McCauley calls a "two-pyramid" approach.

The first pyramid is the "opinion pyramid." This opinion pyramid represents the earlier view of a radicalization process. At the base of this pyramid are those who do not care about a political cause (neutral). Yet as we move higher up the pyramid (as with Moghaddam's steps), individuals are increasingly in support of terrorist action and ideologies. For example, at the next level there are those who believe in the cause but do not justify violence (sympathizers); followed by those who justify violence in defense of the cause (justifiers); and finally, at the top are those who feel it is a "personal moral obligation" to take up violence in defense of the cause. Now, McCauley does not propose this pyramid as a "staircase" or "pathway" because he argues that the pathway is not linear (i.e., someone goes from one stage to another). Instead, individuals can skip levels. What makes it a pyramid is the assumption that the higher up the level, the less overall people who exist at that level (i.e., the more extreme the cognition or behavior, the less people who are engaging in it).

The second pyramid, the "action pyramid," represents the behavioral process of engaging in terrorist behavior. According to McCauley and Moskalenko (2017), at the base of the action pyramid are those who have nothing to do with a political group or cause (inert), above those are individuals who are engaged in legal political action for the cause (activists), and above those are individuals who engage in illegal action for the cause (radicals). Finally, at the apex of the pyramid are those who engage in illegal action that targets civilians (terrorists). Again, the pyramid model is not a linear pathway, and individuals can enter and move between the layers as they so wish. The main implication is that the higher the level of the pyramid, the less individuals there are at that level.

The two-pyramid model that McCauley and Moskalenko propose represents a fundamental truth in human behavior, that the link between thought and action is not always linear and indeed is not a predictable process. In many cases our thoughts do not lead us, and behavior is not merely the culmination of a linear process of increasingly committed cognitions. That said, it is worth mentioning that this strength is also a weakness of the two pyramids approach. While we acknowledge that individuals can move freely between the many layers of both pyramids, what is less certain is the relationship between the two pyramids. For example, it is widely known that someone can be at the very top of the opinion pyramid (the belief that violence is absolutely necessary) while being at the bottom of the action pyramid (i.e., they are engaged in zero terrorist behavior) At the same time, someone can be at the top of the action pyramid without having the opinion that violence is needed or justified.

A QUEST FOR SIGNIFICANCE

One of the main reasons why we have so often relied on the opinion pyramids to explain why people become involved in terrorism stems from the way in which we often studied the problem. Now, it is a long story to tell, and others have recently told it far better than I can here (I recommend the reader look at the work of Bart Schuurman), but I mentioned earlier that terrorism is not the easiest topic to study because it is clandestine by nature. But when people do get access to a sample of individuals who have been engaged in terrorism, the question that the researcher asks them holds huge implications for how people describe their decision to engage. As Horgan (2011, p. 196) outlined in his reflections from the field, "asking a former terrorist about how they became involved with a movement as opposed to why yields different kinds of answers." The same is true of many behavioral outcomes. If I were to ask my sister (a renowned pediatrician in the United Kingdom) why she is a doctor, I would perhaps get an answer in line with egalitarian philosophy and the societal importance of providing care to those who need it most. On the other hand, if I were to ask how she became involved in medicine, she may talk about the fact that our father and mother (also pediatricians)[21] put a toy medicine box in her hand when she was five. Hence the wording of the question can often help tease out the difference between the ideological narrative of a behavior and the underlying process that governs it. The same is true in terrorism; ask someone why they are involved, and you are likely to get an answer that expresses the ideological justification. Ask how and a far more nuanced picture emerges that shows the social, personal, environmental, and even sometimes developmental factors that played a part in their eventual decision to become involved in terrorism (in fact in the next chapter I will outline a case, "Sarah," and you can see the immense complexity of the process of becoming involved in terrorism). This idea was later conceptualized by Horgan as the difference between the "big" and the "small" motivations. Big motivations are the geopolitical issues that drive an ideology and provide the narrative (US foreign policy, domestic abortion policies, environmental concerns, and so on), but underneath all of these big global motivations are the deeply personal "small" motivations that truly drive action.

With this knowledge in hand, and largely spurred by the early work of psychologists such as Max Taylor, we begin to get a far more humanistic understanding of the process of why people become involved in terrorism, and this allows us to unpack both the immense individualization of the process, as well as the psychological universals that may guide behavior. Take, for example, the Newburgh four (the case outlined earlier). Each individual here was involved for a range of different reasons. Some were (perhaps) driven by money, some had a more criminogenic goal and wanted to be involved in the excitement of shooting guns. Laguerre Payen, a mentally ill individual struggling in life, was there (potentially) for the free food, shelter, and perhaps camaraderie that comes from being part of a group striving for something.

This latter point leads me to one last theory to present in this chapter – the idea that the motivation to be involved in terrorism stems from a need for significance. The quest for significance was proposed by Arie Kruglanski and presents a model of radicalization that rests on the central premise that involvement in terrorism provides a route to achieve personal significance. In this theory there are three general drivers of violent extremism: a need for significance, a narrative that provides a means to achieve significance, and a network of like-minded individuals who make the violence-justifying cognitions perceived as morally acceptable. The theory holds that central to all action is the desire to matter, to "be someone," and to have meaning in one's life. Furthermore, this need for significance underlies violent extremism the same way it underlies pro-social behaviors.

The quest for significance model argues that underlying all forms of engagement in terrorist activity exists a general motivational force for significance. This force is not unique to terrorists; in fact, it is human nature to seek significance. Now, in most cases we get significance from roles we hold in our lives (father, son, husband, employee, team member). Our behavioral outlets provide us a sense of significance, which provides satisfaction. By this logic, the absence of a feeling of significance then leads to efforts to gain significance. In this theory, the earliest stages of the radicalization process outlined earlier (such as a deprivation or injustice) actually cause a loss of significance, which in turn create a quest for significance. This can occur at the individual level or the group level (a feeling that someone's social group has lost significance through deprivation). Once someone is looking for significance, it is a terrorist ideology that provides them a means to achieve significance through engaging in violence. Evidence for the importance of significance abounds. Asne Seierstad, the author of One of Us: The Story of Anders Breivik and the Massacre in Norway, wrote about Breivik:

> I always thought that Mr. Breivik was at his most dangerous before we got to know who he was, when all we had was the photo-shopped photographs he had posted online, the ones where he looked tall and well-built, blond and Aryan, posing with his gun.
>
> Mr. Breivik wanted fame. He wanted his 1,500-page cut-and-paste manifesto to be read widely, and he wanted a stage – his trial in Oslo. He called the bomb he set off outside the prime minister's office in Oslo, and the massacre he carried out on the island of Utoya, his "book launch." He told the Norwegian court he had estimated how many people he needed to kill to be read. He had figured a dozen, but ended up killing 77.

It is clear here that his actions sought to provide him a sense of significance that he felt he could not achieve elsewhere. Empirical research with terrorist offenders has also supported the importance of losing significance as a motivator for terrorism. A survey of members of the

Liberation Tigers of Tamil Eelam (a militant separatist group fighting for an independent homeland for Hindu Tamils in Northeastern Sri Lanka) conducted by Kruglanski and colleagues (2014) found that feelings of shame and anger in the preceding weeks predicted correlated with both their support and engagement in violent activities. Again, looking back at the Newburgh four, we can easily see how engagement with Hussain and the plot, while different for each of them, provided a sense of significance that was perhaps lacking in their current lives living in the ghetto of Newburgh.

CONCLUSIONS

In the field of terrorism studies there was recently an argument, started by Marc Sageman (who is one of the central figures in the field and has been studying the phenomena for several decades), about the degree to which the field has "stagnated" (i.e., not moved, or made any progress). Sageman (2014, p. 565) argued that,

> Despite over a decade of government funding and thousands of newcomers to the field of terrorist research, we are no closer to answering the simple question of "What leads a person to turn to political violence?" . . . This has led to an explosion of speculations with little empirical grounding in academia, which has the methodological skills but lacks data for a major breakthrough. Most of the advances in the field have come from historical archival research and analysis of a few field interviews.

His characterization of the field naturally led to an intense debate and indeed several strong rebukes. But while many (myself included) would argue that we are not stagnant, we still have not been able to answer the simple question of "What leads a person to turn to political violence?" And the reason for that is simple: this is not a simple question to answer. We wish it was, and in the early days, researchers thought it was. Several theories were proposed by academics (and even the New York Police Department) that put engaging in terrorism

as the fundamental final stage of a process of increasingly radicalized thoughts that were centered around a political ideology. And if
this were true, so too is the solution; whoever has the most extreme
thoughts is the most likely to be involved in terrorism. In the same
vein, changing their opinion about an ideology will stop them from
being involved. Alas, as with all human behavior, the reality is far
more complex. Instead of a linear radicalization process governing
involvement in terrorism, we have two processes (pyramids); one
is thought-based and discusses how people can adopt and increasingly accept the view that violence is required to achieve a political
goal. But there is a second process, a far more complicated process
that is, to varying degrees, the result of a myriad of experiences and
influences that exist within a person's ecological niche. Similar to the
way we conceptualize other criminal behaviors (such as sex offend-
ing), the factors that govern the behavioral process of undertaking
terrorist action long proceed the emergence of an ideology and a
cognitive shift and in some cases occur without a cognitive shift ever
preceding action. It is this behavioral process that psychologists are
increasingly attempting to conceptualize, and in doing so we have
(perhaps) settled the perspective that engaging in terrorism can be
explained through processes that govern general behavior, rather than
unique or new perspectives. Hence, why theories such as the quest
for significance resonate so profoundly through the field is because
terrorism is the result of a core human psychological process that is
based on the individuals' social and environmental experiences and
influences and leads them to believe that terrorist behavior satisfies a
psychological need.

4

CAN PEOPLE STOP BEING TERRORISTS?

On November 29, 2019, five people were attacked (two fatally) at an offender rehabilitation conference being held in Central London. The offender (Usman Khan) got up in the middle of the conference, wearing a fake suicide vest which he threatened to detonate and began stabbing conference goers and workers with knives that were taped to his hands. He fled into the street where he was restrained by the public until a stand-off with the police during which he was shot dead.

On February 2, 2020, a man armed with a knife and wearing a fake explosive device strapped to his body was shot and killed by the police in South London on Sunday after he was suspected of stabbing people. The attacker, Sudesh Amman, was shot dead by police who were called to the scene. In total, he injured three people, none of them fatally.

The London Bridge attacker, Usman Khan, was previously part of a group that had plotted to bomb the city's stock exchange. He was sentenced to an indeterminate detention for "public protection" and a minimum jail term of eight years. The sentence would have allowed him to be kept in prison beyond the minimum term, had the authorities deemed it necessary. In reference to Khan (and his fellow defendants), the trial judge said:

> In my judgement, these offenders would remain, even after a lengthy term of imprisonment, of such a significant risk that the

public could not be adequately protected by their being managed on license in the community, subject to conditions, by reference to a preordained release date.[1]

In the first few months of his sentence, Khan was upgraded to a "high risk" prisoner. In the second attack, the attacker, Sudesh Amman, had been released one week beforehand after serving half of a three-year sentence for terror offenses. Amman pleaded guilty in November 2018 to six charges of possessing documents containing terrorist information and seven charges of disseminating terrorist publications. He was in possession of manuals about knife fighting and was under active police surveillance at the time of the attack.

While all acts of terrorism are reprehensible, what raised so many questions about these cases was the fact that in both instances the individual who undertook the attack had been released from prison after already serving time for terrorist offenses. The results of these incidents were intense public debate. This debate centered on two issues: the first is a United Kingdom policy of early release (allowing people to be released before completing their entire sentence); the second issue is how, if at all, someone who has been involved in terrorism can ever be a safe member of society. It is this second question that we will focus on in this chapter.

DETAINMENT VS. DERADICALIZATION

The cases presented earlier reinvigorated the discussion around "what do we do with someone who is convicted of terrorism?" And of course, similar to the wider question of how do we treat people who have committed a crime, the issue spans philosophical questions of if we should seek to deradicalize them, legal questions of how long they should spend in prison (in relation to the seriousness of their crime), and more practical and security-related concerns such as if prison might (counter-intuitively) make the problem worse. Even the briefest discussion on the topic will show how intertwined and complex the problem is. Take, for example, the following segment which was featured in a panel interview on *Good Morning Britain* in the week after the South London attack. The extract that follows covers one to two minutes of conversation, but we can already see the issues presented earlier coming to the fore:

SUSANNA REID: Should all convicted terrorists be given a life sentence? Or should the focus be on rehabilitation and deradicalization, and does that work?

PIERS MORGAN: Joining us now is journalist Carole Malone who says terrorists should be imprisoned for life, Dr. Usman Hasan, a terrorism expert who says deradicalization does work, and former prisoner Chris Atkins, who witnessed radicalization while in jail but thinks a longer sentence goes against democracy.

We have a system in this country [the United Kingdom] where over 70 criminals at the moment are on life without parole, full life, they will never come out. And these include the killers of Lee Rigby [see Chapter 1], for example, who were radicalized. And yet we seem to treat terrorists like the one who committed the outrageous attack in Streatham [Sudesh Amman] on Sunday, in a different way. We view them as somehow less dangerous.

CAROLE MALONE: I keep on hearing stories and talking to people about this, who say "Yeah, well he was only in there for three years, he hadn't actually done something." Well, that's not strictly true because when he was arrested by police he was found with a cache of weapons. He was found with an air gun, he was found with a knife, he was found with an ISIS flag. He had encouraged his girlfriend to behead her parents and had said over periods of years that "he wanted to die," that his fantasy was to die as a terrorist. You know we all read what his mum said, and she said he was a good boy, and he was radicalized in Belmont (the prison where he served his first term). No, he wasn't, he was a convicted terrorist when he went in there.

PIERS MORGAN: He probably got further radicalized. Our prison system is so dysfunction[al] that actually it makes things worst. So, what do we do about that?

CAROLE MALONE: Well we have got to do more than we are doing because the deradicalization program we are doing does not work. Usman Khan had been on two of those de-radicalization programs. He was the poster boy for de-radicalization, and it didn't work and various prison bosses have said that terrorists inside are using them as a "get out of jail free card" because you enroll in them to make it look like you want to change, and you don't want to change, and Usman Khan the minute he came out, committed offenses.

SUSANNA REID: Dr. Usman Hassan, when two prisoners remain radicalized having been released, what evidence is there that de-radicalization works? Those are two examples, but have you got a counter-balance?

DR. USMAN HASAN: We have dozens of successful de-radicalization cases, dozens, hundreds, tens of thousands around the world. There are dozens, Ramzi Muhammad, 21/7 plotter, Jordan Horner, former ISIS plotter. There are many, many, we just don't hear about their stories.

SUSANNA REID: If someone's mindset was once, you know, "I want to be a jihadi, and I want to fight this holy war," what is it that you are saying to people in order to de-radicalize them?

DR. USMAN HASAN: Well, my colleagues and I have actually de-radicalized dozens of young men and women. You know, I was once a jihadi when I was 19; you know I took part in jihad in Afghanistan, against the communists, that was different then, way before 9/11, but I know the mindset, many of my colleagues know the mindset, but it's basically growing up and kind of giving them a bit of love actually.

CAROLE MALONE: You're saying coddle a terrorist? Seriously?

PIERS MORGAN: Out of interest, why should we show these people any love?

SUSANNA REID: Well because they keep radicalizing!

DR. USMAN HASAN: This guy was 18, he was a kid basically.

PIERS MORGAN: Well, he may be a kid, but he is also a kid who got out of prison and within days tried to stab people to death.

DR. USMAN HASAN: Yeah, but that's because of the naivety and our short sentences. The system's naivety that he was let out so early.

There is a lot to unpack in the very brief exchange presented here, and many of the soundbites, or small phrases, represent both ideological and societal opinions on the topic. Take, for example, the comment by Piers Morgan: "Out of interest, why should we show these people any love?" and Carole Malone, "You're saying coddle a terrorist? Seriously?" Both of these represent a belief that terrorists are not *deserving* of rehabilitation, especially if that rehabilitation involves the delivery of positive affect. You also heard the suggestion that prisoners' game the deradicalization "system" and use it as a way to minimize their sentence by feigning deradicalization intent. It is perhaps this suggestion that also led to the announcement of the UK government that it was going to introduce lie detectors as part of a new package of measures to make more informed choices about who can and cannot be released.[2]

Dr. Hasan, on the other hand, not only believes that deradicalization works and that there are dozens of domestic cases, and thousands of global cases, but he also understands the process of deradicalization because of his own experiences as a youth. At the same time, Morgan (and indeed Malone) seem to support the idea of a permanent life sentence, even for those who have not committed any harm but have shown terrorist intent. The counterargument to this, however, is (1) the democratic implications of significantly increasing sentence time consummate to criminal deed, and (2) the suggestion (mentioned in passing, but elaborated on later in the interview) that radicalization in prison is a significant problem. This view holds that individuals convicted of low-level terrorist activity who *could* be deradicalized end up becoming more of a threat after a stint in prison.

In this short discussion, too, there is one further point that warrants our attention, which, as we shall see, is central to the problem. When Dr. Hasan is asked *how* people are deradicalized, his answer is that "it's basically growing up and kind of giving them a bit of love actually." Now, in the previous chapter the definition of radicalization provided by McCauley and Moskalenko (2017, p. 415) was a "change in beliefs, feelings, and behaviors in directions that increasingly justify intergroup violence and demand sacrifice in defense of the ingroup." But in Dr. Hasan's conceptualization of deradicalization, he emphasizes the need for love and growing up. Even in this passing sentence, we see the fragility of understanding around what we are actually trying to achieve because if deradicalization is the reverse of radicalization, then by default it should be a change in beliefs, feelings, and behaviors in directions that *decreasingly* justify intergroup violence and demand sacrifice in defense of the ingroup. In this sense deradicalization is exactly the same as radicalization in that it represents a cognitive shift in mindset. Yet, when we talk about it in the real world, we often conflate it with the wider process of being engaged in terrorism (or not).

In this chapter we unpack these two psychological processes (cognitive and behavioral) associated with leaving terrorism, as well as provide a case study of deradicalization in action to show (1) the immense complexity of the process, (2) the fact that deradicalization is a natural extension of the process of involvement, and (3) that we can separate the cognitive and behavioral processes of leaving terrorism (spoiler alert: it is the stopping the behavior that matters far more than stopping the cognitions).

REVERSE RADICALIZATION?

In 2008, in a TIME magazine special focus on "Future Revolutions," "reverse radicalization" was listed as number four. The idea is simple: while psychologists had preoccupied themselves with the search for why people become a terrorist, they had yet to look at an equally important question: how does someone decide to stop being a terrorist? This question has often been focused on by academics who seek to identify the psychological process of leaving terrorism, but, similar to the previous chapter, they often conflated the process of leaving terrorism with the process of deradicalization. This is why the first issue with understanding if, how, and why someone leaves terrorism is to *define* what leaving terrorism actually means; only then can we seek to understand the process as a whole.

So, if, as in the previous chapter, we adopt a two-pyramid model of becoming involved in terrorism – one is cognitive (radicalization) and one is behavioral (engaging in terrorism behavior) – then we can conceptualize leaving terrorism as the reverse of the same two pyramids; one is cognitive (deradicalization) and one is behavioral (disengaging in terrorist behavior). And again, as with the two-pyramid model proposed by McCauley and Moskalenko, these two pyramids can operate relatively independently of each other and, just like in the previous chapter, it is the behavioral outcome of no longer engaging in terrorist behavior that is of utmost concern.

In the early 2010s, a team of researchers led by John Horgan and Mary-Beth Altier, then at the International Center for the Study of Terrorism (ICST), began a project aimed at understanding the factors, pathways, and processes that underpin how, why, when, and where individuals disengage from terrorist groups. The project lasted for several years, and new findings and theories from this data continue to be published to this day.[3] Overall this project (along with some seminal early work on the topic by Albert Bandura, Tore Bjørgo, and concurrent work by other leading scholars such as Daniel Koehler, Peter Simi, and Fernando Reinares) allowed us to make four clear statements about the behavioral process of leaving terrorism behind:[4]

1 The process of disengaging is directly related to the process of engaging in that the motivations for becoming involved can directly influence motivations for leaving.
2 The process of disengaging is the result of a series of push and pull factors that act as forces on the individual; some factors pull the individual away from the group, while others push them out.
3 The process is dynamic and involves multiple stages but can happen instantly for some while slowly over many years for others.
4 Disengagement involves a physical process (separating from the group) and a psychological process (psychologically not wanting to engage in terrorism anymore). Both are separate (i.e., you can have one without the other), but the emergence of one can facilitate the other.

To better demonstrate these overall findings, it would be useful to examine a real-life case of terrorist disengagement. The purpose of this case is to humanize the process of leaving terrorism and to show how many of the psychological processes involved are just reflections of core human psychological processes, just in a different context. So let us look at the case of "Sarah." Sarah's story was collected as part of the original ICST project and was later published by Horgan, Altier and colleagues in full.[5]

SARAH'S STORY

HOW SARAH BECAME INVOLVED IN TERRORISM

Sarah's account of becoming involved in terrorism emphasizes a range of factors rather than a singular event. Sarah was raised by a Baptist father and a Catholic mother. Despite an emphasis on religious schooling, she realized early how this focus on religion clashed with her parents' nonreligious lifestyle. Both smoked, and Sarah described both as alcoholics. This, unsurprisingly, "was always kind of a confusing kind of thing." Sarah also disclosed how she felt that her parents held "old-fashioned armchair prejudices." She recalled her mother had a saying, "You're my child, and I love you unconditionally. There's not anything you could ever do to make me love you less, but you better never bring home a [racial slur]."

The reasons for Sarah's initial interest in violent extremism were complicated. From an early age Sarah was involved in a wide array of antisocial behaviors. She attributed this behavior, in part, to a specific reaction to her acrimonious and often turbulent relationship with her father:

> I [felt] unwanted by my father. I wanted to, you know, feel loved and like I was important. And it, at that age, um, that was in my eyes a way to do that. And it didn't dawn on me that I was feeling worse the more I did, you know, the more I slept around, the more drugs, more drinking.

As Sarah reached puberty, she began to develop a sexual interest in other girls. This confusion was amplified by her religious upbringing, and she felt it exacerbated her growing torment. When Sarah first came into contact with a right-wing group, "[I] had all of this built up. The prejudice, the religious confusion, the sexual orientation confusion. I was angry, because when my parents divorced, my father did not care about my sister and I."

Sarah's first exposure to the extreme right-wing scene came via a group of skinheads in high school. Sarah says that, in hindsight, these skinhead groups were little more than "watered down punk rockers" mostly focused around the "style, the way of life, the music scene." This skinhead group eventually split into neo-Nazi and antiracist factions. Sarah continued to affiliate with the neo-Nazi faction because,

> It was kind of that anger and that violence when I started out that kind of made it very easy for me to fall in with them. Um, the groups themselves were so scattered down there that there was, you know, the group of skinheads that went the racist route. And they would make their own little groups. You know, they would pretty much go to, you know, the corner store or the library or, you know, copy place and make their own fliers and literature and stuff like that. But like I said, that wasn't the initial draw.

SARAH'S FIRST ENGAGEMENT IN TERRORISM

As she continued to engage with the older group, Sarah got more neo-Nazi tattoos and made overt displays of her ties to right-wing violent extremism. It was during her engagement with this older right-wing group that Sarah was exposed to right-wing literature. She emphasized that its significance was less relevant in terms of her indoctrination and far more influential in terms of empowering and equipping her to demonstrate knowledge to impress others. Sarah described in detail the wide range of activities in which she was involved, from recruiting friends into the movement to starting new factions focused on increasing female engagement to engaging in criminal activities and right-wing violence that eventually led to her arrest and incarceration.

HOW SHE DISENGAGED

Sarah recalled that shortly after becoming involved in the extreme right-wing scene, she began having doubts about her involvement. She struggled with recurring conflict about the reality of her involvement, asking herself: "You are a [expletive], why are you doing this?" These doubts usually stemmed from actions she performed that ran contrary to the ideology of the group. Sarah became involved in a relationship with a Hispanic man while at the same time continuing to deepen her commitment to the group. External events also compounded her doubts. The aftermath of the 1995 Oklahoma City bombing caused Sarah to reflect deeply on her entire involvement with the extreme right-wing movement. She struggled with reconciling the knowledge of who committed this act (an extreme right-wing actor) with the infamous photograph of a one-year-old infant's bloodied, dirtied body being carried away by a firefighter:

> I think it, it finally started to seep into my conscious mind, you know, like "What are you doing? Do you want to be the bomber? Do you want to be, you know, that person that, that does this? Is it worth it? Is, you know, this the ultimate price I'm going to end up paying for what I'm doing?" And there were those times that I would have, you know, the little voice in my head saying "You're a [expletive]. You know, there's something better." But I would always do more drugs, drink more, become more involved to kind of, you know, push those thoughts away.

While struggling to cope with deepening disillusionment, Sarah began to fear that others in the group might detect her efforts at concealment. In response, she notes that she felt an urgent need to demonstrate renewed commitment:

I literally made a point to go out and recruit more people and, you know, to be more hardcore and start more fights. And, you know, because I felt "Now I have to re-prove myself because they knew that I faltered."

Sarah eventually admitted to herself that she was disillusioned with her involvement, yet the absence of attractive alternatives, coupled with her lack of confidence, presented obstacles that prevented her from walking away. She acknowledged that she lacked "the resources" to leave. Despite the negative consequences of continued involvement, to her the group still provided self-worth, validation, and protection.

If I . . . had the resources I probably would have been able to leave. But in the end I said, you know, "I can't do it. I'm on house arrest, where can I go. I have no money, I can't move." You know, I, um, I can't protect my family, and I still very much wanted that attention.

Certain singular moments were essential to her disengagement. One evening Sarah was hanging out with other members of her group when she ended up aiding an armed robbery of a store. The owner was severely beaten. Fearing arrest and prosecution for the crime, Sarah went on the run. She felt she could not "keep doing this forever," because at some point, she was "going to have to start popping out babies." On a few occasions, she gathered all of her belongings and went to the bus station but stopped at the last minute because she had a "fear of being alone" and "horrible low self-esteem." But in the end, it was federal prison that "changed her life":

One thing I often see is the people in the movement, you're so preoccupied with, you know, keeping up the beliefs and all that that you almost need . . . prison gives you a space, like gives you a time to, to sort of think about those things . . . and entertain [those thoughts].

Prison allowed Sarah to interact with a racially diverse population. Sarah recalled that everyone

> knew what I was, and they still treated me like any other person. And there were a couple of, you know, white women I became friends with. But I actually ended up being the closest with [black] women for whatever reason.

In prison Sarah also realized that she could achieve a sense of self-worth and belonging outside of her involvement in right-wing violent extremism. Sarah was assigned to help with a General Education Development (GED) program; she taught women (of all different races) how to read, and these positive experiences had a profound effect on her:

> It was more for me than them. That, to know that I had that power within me, that I was capable of, you know, being compassionate and empathetic and, you know, actually caring about people that I professed to hate for so many years – those kind of experiences changed me tremendously.

These experiences allowed Sarah to leave the group, and remain disengaged after prison:

> You know, I went to prison this racist, horrible, violent person, and my whole life changed. It was like being reborn but not in like the religious sense. When I came out of prison, you know, like I experienced things differently. The colors looked brighter, you know. . . . I became comfortable with the fact that I may not be heterosexual.

Sarah's case is a clear example of what "becoming a terrorist" means. It is not simple nor linear. It is complex. It involves multiple pushes and pulls. Furthermore, these pushes and pulls changed over time. They evolved, as did Sarah (or perhaps "grew up" as Dr. Hasan said at the start of the chapter). Now rather than seek to understand her trajectory here, what is critical to emphasize is that it is very clear that "radicalization" was not the problem, nor was "deradicalization" alone the solution. Did she engage in radical violence? Yes. But was the cause of that simply a process of adopting and adhering to an extreme right ideology? Of course not. Let us go through the four statements made earlier about disengagement so that we can see each point in practice through Sarah. In doing so, we will also emphasize what the study of disengagement as a whole has found (rather than simply extrapolating a process from a single case).

1 **The process of disengaging is directly related to the process of engaging in that the motivations for becoming involved can directly influence motivations for leaving.**

In her exploration of the criminal motivation, Youngs (2006) argued that the specific nature of someone's criminal behavior reflects underlying incentives that they have for their action. Now, this may seem logical on the face of it (we do things that fulfil basic needs and human incentives), but if you look at the way in which we talk about the theories of radicalization, we see that the cognitive change predicts the willingness and motivation to be involved in terrorism, but there is no integration of the nature of behavior that is engaged in. As we showed in Chapter 3, people engage in terrorism in very different ways and that this is usually an extension of what they wanted to achieve through being involved. In Sarah's case, we can see that some of her core drives were a need for acceptance and self-worth and that this was provided by being involved in this group. This idea then reflects itself in the type of behavior in which she engaged, those behaviors that provided her a sense of acceptance and self-worth. She got tattoos, actively recruited members, became engaged in violence. What is interesting though is that we can extend the role of these motivations to engage and see that they also impact motivations to disengage. In the case of Sarah, when she realized she could gain fulfillment from other actions (such as teaching others), the psychological benefits of being involved in the group were no longer there. What this means then is that once the *needs* (or significance) that the group provided could be acquired elsewhere, the pull toward the group was no longer as powerful.

2 **The process of disengaging is the result of a series of push and pull factors that act as opposing forces; some factors pull the individual away from the group, while others push them out.**

One of the most consistent findings from those who study disengagement and deradicalization is that disillusionment is an important psychological experience. Tore Bjørgo (2011) argues that the failure to achieve what people expected or dreamed about is usually the source of disillusionment, and subsequently, a main reason to disengage from violent extremism. A clear example of this is the spate of young individuals who left the United States and Europe to join ISIS. After the original movement of young individuals (as many as 250 from the United States tried to leave), there began to be an increasing number of people wanting to return home, and increasingly it was because they had become disillusioned with the realities of the life that they had left for. In their review of the narratives of 58 defectors who had also left ISIS, Peter Neumann, director of the International Centre for the Study of Radicalization and Political Violence (ICSR; Neumann, 2016), found that four key narratives emerged:

1 "IS is more interested in fighting fellow (Sunni) Muslims than the Assad government."
2 "IS is involved in brutality and atrocities against (Sunni) Muslims."
3 "IS is corrupt and un-Islamic."
4 "Life under IS is harsh and disappointing."

These factors represent just a few of the push and pull factors that have elsewhere been identified as influencing somebody's decision to disengage with terrorism.

Although there is no universal single reason why individuals turn away from terrorism, researchers have explored personal narratives (either through interviews or autobiographies) to identify the "push" and "pull" factors that make disengagement more likely (e.g., Bjørgo, 2009; Altier et al., 2017). Some of the factors that push individuals away from terrorism are when they have unmet expectations, they become disillusioned with members or the strategy of the group (this is seen in the ISIS fighters studied by Neumann), they have difficulties adjusting to the clandestine lifestyle, or the psychological trauma they experience from engaging in violence (or facilitating groups that engage in violence) becomes too much for them. Those factors that pull them away are often positive experiences outside the group, employment or educational demands, or a desire to marry and have a family (Sarah reflected this pull factor). While the specific mix of these disengagement variables will of course vary depending on the individual, the group, the time, and the situation, there are some disengagement variables that are more prevalent than others. Recently, Mary-Beth Altier, John Horgan, Emma Leonard, and I analyzed autobiographies from individuals who had left an extremist group and had chosen to write about their experiences. In total, we (and by "we" I mean a workforce of trained student interns at the International Center for the Study of Terrorism) analyzed 87 autobiographies and identified 170 unique disengagement events (meaning an event where an individual left the terrorist group). For each of these events we coded the factors that they *said* impacted their decision to leave and if, in their own words, that factor played a large or small role. In terms of push factors, disillusionment with the strategy or actions of the group was the main reason people voluntarily decided to leave a terrorist group behind. The next most common push factor was disillusionment, specifically with the leaders of the group. Loss of faith in the ideology was only the fifth most prevalent factor, followed by burnout, fear of being caught, fear of being a victim of violence oneself, and difficulty coping with the lifestyle and violent nature of terrorism. For pull factors, the desire to seek employment was cited in just over 15% of the cases of voluntary disengagement, followed by the desire to dedicate more time to family, and issues of balancing family life with the demands of being involved in terrorism. These findings show both the diversity of the factors that to varying degrees influence an individual's decision to disengage.

3 **The process is dynamic and involves multiple stages but can happen instantly for some while slowly over many years for others.**

We learn something else from Sarah's process of disengaging from terrorism; it is not dissimilar to the everyday human experience of disengaging from anything. I want you to imagine, for a moment, a time when you *disengaged* from something. It could be a relationship, a job, a hobby, or even a social group. When you look back at that processes, was it immediate, or did it take you some time to decide to leave? Did you experience a triggering event and then begin a cascade of cognitions that led to your eventual decision? These all are natural human processes to which we are subject when making large decisions, and they are reflected in the decision to disengage from terrorism. One of the most prominent models that is often applied to the field is Ebaugh's (1988) theory of "role exit." Based on 185 in-depth interviews that she conducted with individuals who had disengaged from previously identified roles (e.g., spouse, clergy, prostitute, alcoholic, convict), Ebaugh noted that disengagement begins with initial doubts that then cause the individual to question and reconsider their role. This process of doubt leads to a slow decrease in the perceived satisfaction that they receive from the role and a fundamental realignment of their commitment (in that the benefits of commitment may no longer outweigh the costs). After experiencing doubts, individuals begin to seek and weigh alternatives. They begin to evaluate the degree to which they can realistically hold another role, and the potential benefits of that role in comparison to their current role. In those instances where individuals believe they have a viable alternative, they may decide to exit. This is a significant turning point and usually involves a behavioral step to solidify the exit (e.g., handing in a letter of resignation). Finally, after leaving, the individual must construct a new identity and find satisfaction in this in order to stop them from being pulled back into their old role. Now, while these stages present as a nice linear model (doubts, alternate search, deciding to leave, exit and new role, post-exit socialization), the experience of these stages can be very different. Some people can go through the process in an immensely quick time, while others may take years or decades. Some may start the process, but eventually end up staying engaged and satisfied. But what we learn from the model is that leaving is a process, and with the case of Sarah (and other cases of disengagement collected from psychologists), disengagement from terrorism follows a similar pattern to the general process of leaving something behind. We have doubts, these doubts grow, and we seek alternatives; at one point we have to commit to leaving, and once we have left, we need to craft a new identity that is shaped by our new role and provides as much (or more) satisfaction than the role that was just left behind. This is why disengaging from terrorism is a far more complex science than simply "deradicalizing" people, because engagement in terrorism, and hence disengaging from terrorism, is tied to much more than just ideology; it is shaped by our values, identity, and psychological needs, and all of these factors must be met in a new role in order for someone to choose to disengage.

4 **Disengagement involves a physical process (separating from the group) and a psychological process (psychologically not wanting to engage in terrorism anymore). Both are separate (i.e., you can have one without the other), but the emergence of one can facilitate the other.**

As we stated earlier, as with engagement in terrorism, for disengagement, too, we must adopt a two-pyramid model that includes both a cognitive change and a behavioral one. What we see in the case presented earlier is that, as with engagement in terrorism, these pyramids operate relatively independently of each other. In reality this means that an individual can cognitively want to leave a terrorist organization but at the same time still physically be engaged in terrorist behavior. We see this in Ebaugh's model of role exit in that while someone may have psychologically disengaged from the group and is no longer satisfied with their role, they may not decide to leave because of a lack of suitable alternatives. Sarah's case showed this dynamic in that while she was keen to leave the group, she was unable to fund and take care of herself, leaving her no other option. However, what we did see was that the forced physical separation from the group (through imprisonment) provided Sarah with the opportunity to fully work through the process of disengaging from terrorism and find and accept a new role. This dynamic interplay between physical and psychological disengagement has been reported by other psychologists who have focused on the role of prison as an important avenue to become completely disengaged. One example of this is a case collected by John Horgan and colleagues as part of this same disengagement project. The individual, "Ahmed," recalled how he had joined a terrorist organization at the age of 15 with "absolutely no expectations" about what his involvement would entail. Over time he began to have doubts about his involvement, but he could not leave. He felt the leaders of the groups were psychopaths ("From that moment I realized there were some people in control here who were complete psychopaths"), but he was trapped because his role in attacks had led to the possibility of forensic evidence existing that could be used against him if he left the group. But finally, when Ahmed was arrested, he felt relief:

> I remember when I was arrested and was in the police station, when the police were trying to interrogate me, they didn't realize that there was this – it was like a Niagara Falls of relief – and my mind went into this cool zone of intense relief because as I was sitting there, my mind far away from the interrogation, taking no part in it whatsoever, my mind was thinking, "My God, I've

survived, I've been captured, I never expected to. . . ." They must have been wondering why this guy wasn't responding to interrogation at all. I was sitting there going – [expletive] I'm alive. But it's curious with the belief too – it's a sign that people often don't appreciate the fact that the [terrorist] that they've captured may have been looking for a way out.

CONCLUSIONS

The two attacks in the United Kingdom in the late 2010s have reinvigorated the discussion around how, if at all, we can deradicalize terrorist offenders. The implications of the results of this discussion are broad and far-reaching. They range from stronger sentences for terrorist offenders to the incorporation of new (and largely unverified) scientific methods such as the use of "lie detectors" to judge a person's intentions to reoffend prior to release.[6] In this chapter I hope to have communicated a few basic truths. First, the process of leaving terrorism is both behavioral and cognitive. While we can call (though many will argue) the cognitive process of wanting to no longer be a terrorist "deradicalization" (though this assumes they were radicalized to begin with; see Chapter 3), there is a behavioral process of disengaging from terrorism on which our attention must be focused. Second, disengaging is the result of a series of factors that both push the person away from wanting to be involved in terrorism and pull them toward wanting not to be involved in terrorism. There are myriad push and pull factors that psychologists have identified that play a role, but the main one is centered on issues of disillusionment and the individual wanting a career or family life outside of the group. Third, the psychological process of leaving reflects a process many of us have gone through in our lives, including doubt, seeking alternatives, and (hopefully) eventually making the decision to leave. This process can take a long time, and some people are unable to complete the process despite *wanting* to leave. And this brings in the last learning point: often despite wanting to leave, the lack of resources, options, and alternatives can lead to someone staying engaged. This last point is especially important when we consider issues such a counter-terrorism, which often emphasizes the punishment that will occur for those who engage in terrorism. So while policies such as removing citizenship from those who left the country to join ISIS may work to deter those from becoming involved, they may also prevent individuals who are currently involved from being able to leave.[7]

5

CAN WE STOP TERRORISM?

In this chapter we look to the problem of countering terrorism. Now, there are many angles this chapter could take; we could go global and look at the wealth of global issues that are (to varying degrees) associated with the spread of terrorism around the world. Issues of poverty, the climate crisis, war, and the economic climate all to varying degrees play a role, and each is a field of study in its own right. At the same time, we could look at this as a tactical problem and discuss the effectiveness of leader decapitation (removing the leader), negotiation, surveillance, policing, and the law. Finally, we could look politically and examine the role of politics in preventing the motivations for engagement in terrorism and terrorist behavior (e.g., climate laws, laws against religious freedoms, and so on). The field of countering terrorism is broad, and there are decades of study associated with each of the variables we have just highlighted. So given the size, scope, and general ethos of this book, instead of stretching our focus too thinly across a broad range of topics, I wanted to discuss a single aspect that psychologists have been focused on that really centers on the psychology of the individual: risk assessment.

How we identify the risk that an individual poses is critical to our ability to identify and intervene in cases of terrorism. It is one of the most central aspects of how we stop the next terrorist attack, and it is closely related to the concepts we focused on in Chapters 2 and 3. In essence, risk assessment is an attempt to *operationalize* what we know about who becomes a terrorist and use that knowledge proactively to predict who will become the *next terrorist*. Thus, risk assessment is a deeply psychological process, and it is an area that in many other domains psychologists have had incredible success. Risk assessment tools have been developed for suicide, depression, inter-partner violence, and many other troublesome behaviors. But a risk assessment for terrorism has long eluded the field.

In order to show both the process and complexity of risk assessment in the real world, this chapter shall focus on a single case to show why, even when looking at a single instance, risk assessment can be so tricky. This case is chosen specifically because it is meant to closely represent what could be viewed as the vast majority of modern terrorist cases – a lone individual, escalating toward a crude, yet effective, operational goal. In fact, this case is even referred to as "A Most American Terrorist."

A MOST AMERICAN TERRORIST: THE MAKINGS OF DYLANN ROOF

In August 2017, in *GQ* (*Gentleman's Quarterly*) magazine, Rachel Kaadzi Ghansah published a profile of white supremacist and mass murderer Dylann Roof, who killed nine parishioners at the historically black Emanuel African Methodist Episcopal Church (Mother Emanuel) in Charleston, South Carolina, in June 2015. The 9,000-word exploration of Roof's origins won a National Magazine Award and Pulitzer Prize for feature writing. In the next section, I shall draw heavily on Ghansah's piece to provide a brief history of the origins, motivation, and psychology of Dylann Roof. The reader is strongly encouraged to spend an hour or so reading the original essay in all its glory.[1]

THE ATTACK

Dylann Roof arrived in Charleston at 7:48 p.m., June 17, 2015. He was armed with a 45-caliber Glock pistol and .88 with hollow-point bullets that he had purchased in the preceding weeks. He drove into the gated parking lot of the Mother Emanuel Church and walked through the basement entrance where 12 members of the Bible study were gathered in the fellowship hall for an evening Bible study.

At first, Roof took part in the Bible study. He asked for and sat next to the senior pastor, State Senator Clementa C. Pinckney. Initially, he listened to others during the study group and engaged in the discussions of scripture. When the participants began praying, he stood up and aimed his gun at one of the fellow worshippers. When another attendee tried to talk him down, he said, "I have to do it. You rape our women, and you're taking over our country. And you have to go." Roof then began to shoot the worshippers.[2] After fatally shooting nine people, Roof walked out the door to his car and fled. He was apprehended at a traffic stop 245 miles away from the church the next day. In his car was a handwritten note with the names of several other churches on it, a Confederate flag, a burned US flag, a gun, an empty box of ammunition, and a laser attachment for a gun that helps with accuracy. Roof confessed to the shootings to both the Charleston police and the FBI, telling investigators that he wanted to start a race war.

Quickly after the attack, a website associated with Roof was discovered under the title "lastrhodesian.com" (the Rhodesian Army had fought against black insurgent armies in the 1960s and 70s to maintain white minority rule over territory that is now Zimbabwe). The site included photos of Roof with a handgun and Confederate battle flag and an unsigned, 2,444-word manifesto authored by Roof. In the manifesto he outlined his motivations and some of the factors that led him to his actions. Following are two excerpts, one from the opening paragraphs and one from the very last.[3]

The event that truly awakened me was the Trayvon Martin case. I kept hearing and seeing his name, and eventually I decided to look him up. I read the Wikipedia article and right away I was unable to understand what the big deal was. It was obvious that Zimmerman was in the right. But more importantly this prompted me to type in the words "black on White crime" into Google, and I have never been the same since that day.

An Explanation

To take a saying from a film, "I see all this stuff going on, and I dont see anyone doing anything about it. And it pisses me off."

To take a saying from my favorite film, "Even if my life is worth less than a speck of dirt, I want to use it for the good of society."

I have no choice. I am not in the position to, alone, go into the ghetto and fight. I chose Charleston because it is most historic city in my state, and at one time had the highest ratio of blacks to Whites in the country. We have no skinheads, no real KKK, no one doing anything but talking on the internet. Well someone has to have the bravery to take it to the real world, and I guess that has to be me.

Unfortunately, at the time of writing I am in a great hurry and some of my best thoughts, actually many of them have been to be left out and lost forever. But I believe enough great White minds are out there already.

Please forgive any typos, I didn't have time to check it.

Five days after the shooting Roof was indicted on 33 federal charges, including 12 counts of committing hate crimes (you will remember in Chapter 1 we noted that Roof was not, legally, convicted of terrorist offenses). On May 24, 2016, the Justice Department announced that Roof would face the death penalty. During the trial, Roof's mental health was a significant topic of focus. There were hundreds of pages of psychiatric evaluations, and it was reported that Roof had intense anxiety that his court-appointed defense attorneys would present evidence supporting that he had a developmental disability or mental illness. In a letter to the courts about his own defense, Roof wrote (in O'Shea and Yan, 2016):

Even now I am not entirely sure what they [his lawyers] are planning to say, and I doubt I will know until they actually say it at my trial, because they don't intend to tell me before then. I only found out they would be presenting a mental health defense a few days prior to writing this letter.

Because I have no real defense, my lawyers have been forced to grasp at straws and to present a pathetic, fraudulent excuse for a defense in my name. They have regularly told me in an aggressive manner that I have no say in my own defense, that my input doesn't matter, and that there is nothing I can do about it.

They are extremely moralistic about death penalty, but unfortunately when it comes to lying they do not have any morals at all. So, almost anything they say should be disregarded and I will go as far as to say that they all, both federal and state, should be disbarred. Don't let them fool you or the court like they've fooled me.

DYLANN ROOF.

When I say I have no real defense, I mean that I have no defense that my lawyers would present or that would be acceptable to the court.

On December 15, 2016, the jury found Roof guilty on all 33 federal counts with which he had been charged. He was sentenced to death on January 10, 2017. That said, the sentence is currently being appealed. The main argument is that the district judge should not have allowed Roof to represent himself during the penalty phase given that he was, at that time, a 22-year-old ninth-grade dropout "who believed his sentence didn't matter because white nationalists would free him from prison after an impending race war" (see Levenson and Burnide, 2020). Roof's appellate lawyers argue that he has been diagnosed with "schizophrenia-spectrum disorder, autism, anxiety, and depression," and sought to eliminate his experienced trial attorneys to stop them from preventing evidence of his mental illness to jurors.[4]

THE SCIENCE OF PREDICTION

When we look that this case, the question we ask ourselves in hindsight is "to what extent could we have predicted, or prevented, Dylann

Roof's behavior?" The idea of this principally is to understand what overt factors could have given indicators to his intent so that we can then begin to look for those factors in others. One of the first efforts to support the issue of risk assessment was conducted by Kebbell and Porter (2012). They proposed a series of psychological factors that would be associated with those who wished to *engage in violent extremism*. These risk factors were split into four sub-categories: "standard risk factors" (high frequency, low predictive utility, such as a super-ordinate non-Western identity or a negative view of Western foreign policy); "moderate risk factors" (indicative of higher risk and more supportive of violence, such as religious beliefs that support violence); "higher risk factors" (those associated with enhanced operational capability such as membership to a radical political group); and "extreme risk factors" (those that show an individual has decided to engage in violent extremism). A similar early effort was the Identifying Vulnerable People tool (IVP; available from www.tacticaldeci sionmaking.org). One of the most popular and well-tested tools that identifies indicators is the Terrorist Radicalization Assessment Protocol-18 (TRAP-18). The TRAP-18 was developed by Meloy (2011) and provides a means by which mental health, intelligence, and law enforcement professionals can organize data on a person of concern and provide a framework for their risk management approach. The TRAP-18 has been identified as an investigative template in order to stress that the tool is not established well enough to be considered an assessment tool (Meloy & Gill, 2016). The TRAP-18 has also been shown to be well suited for lone terrorist offenders.

THE TRAP-18 AND DYLANN ROOF

The TRAP-18 is designed to code for eight proximal warning behaviors (such as pathway, fixation, identification, and last resort) and ten longer-term distal characteristics (such as personal grievance, ideological framing, failure of sexual pair bonding, and mental disorder). Each of these behaviors is coded as "present" or "absent," and if it is present, the individual scores a 1. This means that "risk" is conceptualized as the total number of factors present and therefore a higher score. The very simplistic view therefore is that someone who scores a 5 (five factors present) is a lower risk that someone who scores a 10 (though we would not say they are "double" the risk).

For context here let us outline the indicators that Meloy identified, before applying these to Dylann Roof.

TRAP-18 RISK FACTORS: THE WARNING BEHAVIOR TYPOLOGY

Pathway warning behavior: Research, planning, preparation, or implementation of an attack.

Fixation warning behavior: Increasingly pathological preoccupation with a person or a cause, accompanied by a concurrent deterioration in an individual's social and occupational life.

Identification warning behavior: A psychological desire to be a pseudo- commando, or a close association with weapons or other military or law enforcement paraphernalia. Identifying with previous attackers or assassins or identifying oneself as an agent to advance a particular cause or belief system.

Novel Aggression warning behavior: An act of violence that appears unrelated to any targeted violence pathway, or violence that is committed for the first time.

Energy Burst warning behavior: An increase in the frequency or variety of any noted activities related to the target, even if the activities themselves are relatively innocuous, usually in the days, weeks, or hours before the attack.

Leakage warning behavior: Communication to a third party of an intent to do harm to a target through an attack.

Last Resort warning behavior: Evidence of a "violent action imperative" and "time imperative" to the need for action. This reflects that the subject has decided that there is no other alternative than to be violent toward the target. Sometimes it is triggered by a major loss or anticipated loss.

Directly Communicated Threat warning behavior: The communication of a direct threat to the target or law enforcement beforehand.

TRAP-18 RISK FACTORS: DISTAL CHARACTERISTICS OF THE LONE-ACTOR TERRORIST

Personal Grievance and Moral Outrage: Personal life experience and particular historical, religious, or political events that have caused a grievance or outrage. Grievance is often defined by a major loss in love or work, feelings of anger and humiliation, and the blaming of others. Moral outrage on the other hand is typically a vicarious identification with a group which has suffered, even though the individual has usually not experienced the same suffering.

Framed by an Ideology: Beliefs which justify the intent to commit a terrorist act. It can be a religious belief system, a political philosophy, a secular commitment, a one-issue conflict, or an idiosyncratic justification.

Failure to Affiliate with an Extremist Group: The actual failure and/or rejection of the lone-actor terrorist by a radical or extremist group with which he/she wants to join is a risk factor because in some cases the subject has been rejected by the extremist group because the group is too moderate for him/her.

Dependence on the Virtual Community: Communication with others through social media, chat rooms, emails, lis-servs, texting, tweeting, and so on about radical or extreme beliefs.

Thwarting of Occupational Goals: A major setback or failure in a planned occupational life course.

Changes in Thinking and Emotion: A more simplistic and absolute state of emotions. Emotions typically move from anger and argument to contempt and disdain for others' beliefs to disgust for the out-group and a willingness to homicidally aggress against them.

Failure of Sexual-Intimate Pair Bonding: Historically failing to form a lasting sexually intimate relationship.

Mental Disorder: Evidence of a major mental disorder by history or at present.

Greater Creativity and Innovation: Evidence of tactical thinking "outside the box" (i.e., innovative or creative).

Criminal Violence: Instrumental criminal violence that is separate from the terrorist act.

DYLANN ROOF AND THE WARNING BEHAVIOR TYPOLOGY

Pathway warning behavior: Present (1). From the manifesto found in Roof's car and the one posted online, there is clear evidence that he had researched his attack and target.

Fixation warning behavior: Present (1). Although slightly less clear as it requires an increasing deterioration of social networks, it is possible that elements of the manifesto, and narratives from those around him, support this.

Identification warning behavior: Present (1). Images on the website clearly show Roof with a gun and embracing a "pseudo commando" image. He also identified himself as an advocate for his cause.

Novel Aggression warning behavior: Absent (0). No evidence of any earlier acts of violence.

Energy Burst warning behavior: Absent (0). Only due to a lack of knowledge about Roof's actions on the days preceding the attacks.

Leakage warning behavior: Present (1). There is evidence from Roof's friends that he had leaked a degree of intent to those around him.

Last Resort warning behavior: Present (1). His manifesto demonstrates the mindset that this is a last resort.

Directly Communicated Threat warning behavior: Absent (0). Roof did not directly communicate a threat.

DYLANN ROOF AND THE DISTAL CHARACTERISTICS OF THE LONE-ACTOR TERRORIST

Personal Grievance and Moral Outrage: Present (1). Roof clearly was feeling moral outrage and a personal grievance.

Framed by an Ideology: Present (1). Roof's actions were clearly framed by an ideology.

Failure to Affiliate with an Extremist Group: Absent (0). There is no evidence that Roof failed to affiliate with an extremist group.

Dependence on the Virtual Community: Absent (0). While Roof had an online profile, this seems very much like "one-way traffic" in that he mainly posted and did not have a clear virtual "community."

Thwarting of Occupational Goals: Absent (0). There is no evidence that any occupational goals were thwarted.

Changes in Thinking and Emotion: Absent (0). While tough to determine without knowing more details about his earlier years, there is no evidence that his thinking changed in the immediate period before the attack.

Failure of Sexual-Intimate Pair Bonding: Present (1). To quote Ghansah (2017), "Shortly after Roof was identified as the killer, a story circulated in the press that Dylann had been upset about a white girlfriend who had rejected him for a black boy. But Roof himself denied this in court. There was no girl. In fact, no one, not a single person anywhere, remembers Dylann Roof ever dating anyone."

Mental Disorder: Present (1). At his trial, lawyers cited social anxiety disorder, a mixed substance abuse disorder, a schizoid personality disorder, depression by history, and possible autistic spectrum disorder. However, the specific term is "evidence of," and it is viable that pre-crime there was no evidence of the disorder as he was not, at the time, officially diagnosed.

Greater Creativity and Innovation: Absent (0). It is arguable that there is little creativity in Roof's thinking.

Criminal Violence: Absent (0). At the time of the crime, there was no evidence that Roof was violent, and he had no previous violent convictions.

So overall, in this crude application, Dylann Roof scored 9/18, and the TRAP-18 performed in line with previous performances for example, when Meloy and Gill (2016) applied the TRAP-18 to a sample of lone-actor terrorists, the majority (78%) experienced a grievance, all of them were guided by an ideology, and over 80% had a failed sexual-intimate partner bond and changes in thinking and emotion. In terms of the combination or different risk factors, overall, 70% of the 111 lone actors demonstrated at least half of the TRAP-18 indicators. Dylann Roof would fall into this category. In this sense, we can say that the TRAP-18 worked.

PREDICTION IN THE REAL WORLD

While the TRAP-18 worked in the Dylann Roof case, there is a problem with this form of prediction in the real world because we are not risk assessing individuals in a vacuum. Thus, how well a tool works is based solely on the performance of the tool on one individual and how well the tool performs on a large group of people and how consistently it marks people who have *real* intent (like Dylann Roof) with higher scores than those who have not. We can put this point in perspective by working through an example tool with a real sample.

I would like you to imagine that you work for a security agency, and you are tasked with screening intelligence reports and detecting who is a high risk and needs further attention and who is a low risk and needs less attention. We can imagine you are using a risk assessment tool (like the TRAP-18) and that tool has 90% accuracy in that it correctly identifies the person as high or low risk 90% of the time.

Every day you have 1,000 people to assess, and of this 1,000 people, ten individuals (1%) have "hostile intent." I want you to then imagine that you are working one day, and this tool tells you that the person coming through security has been identified as having "hostile intent" (i.e., they scored very high on the tool).

Right away, I want you to ask yourself a few questions: what is your degree of confidence in this tool? In your mind, what are the chances that this tool has falsely flagged the wrong person? Perhaps you think the accuracy is high, and you are confident this person is high risk. Now, let us evaluate this tool.

When evaluating a tool, there are two main factors that need to be considered (which we discussed before) – sensitivity (the chances that the tool will "flag" the person you are interested in) and specificity (the chances it will not "flag" the people you are not interested in). Now, with the given tool, despite 90% accuracy, it is also inaccurate 90% of the time. While this may seem like a "quantum" issue (Schrödinger's risk assessment, if you will), it is a statistical fact that the tool is wrong nine of the ten times it tells you someone is high risk. To show why, let us calculate the effectiveness of this tool.

So we have 1,000 people, and ten of these people are "terrorists." This means that 990 are not terrorists.

Now, in order to work out the effectiveness of any tool, we need to calculate four numbers.

True positives – The number of times it correctly "flags" someone
False positives – The number of times it incorrectly "flags" someone
True negatives – The number of times it correctly does not flag someone
False negatives – The number of times it incorrectly does not "flag" someone

Here, let's look at these numbers with 90% sensitivity and specificity.

True positives – 9. It will correctly identify nine out of ten individuals (90%)
False positives – 99. It will incorrectly identify 10% of the 990 other individuals (10%)
True negatives – 891. It will correctly identify 891 of the remaining 990 as negatives (90%)
False negatives – 1. It will incorrectly identify one of the ten individuals as negative (10%)

This leaves us with the following 2 x 2 box.

		Actual	
		Intent	No intent
Prediction	Intent	TP	FP
	No intent	FN	TN

In this case this box looks like this:

		Actual		
		Intent	No intent	**Totals**
Prediction	Intent	9	99	108
	No intent	1	891	892
	Totals	10	990	1000

So from here we can calculate the overall accuracy of the tool. Hence, rather than "how many times does my tool correctly flag the person," we now look at "how confident can I be in what my tool tells me?" In order to do this, we need to calculate the positive predictive value (PPV) and the negative predictive value.

For PPV we would need to calculate $TP/(TP + FP)$.

So here the PPV is $(9/108) = .083$

A perfect score is "1," and the further the PPV is from 1, the worse the tool is performing. Here $1 - .083 = .917$, meaning that 91.7% of the time, the model is incorrect when it says that someone is a "hit."

For NPV we would need to calculate $TN/(FN + TN)$.

So here the PPV is $(891/892) = .9988$

This means that 99.88% of the time, the model is correct when it says that someone is not a "hit."

MINIMIZING FALSE POSITIVES?

What we see in this example explains a lot of the problems we have seen throughout this book. You will remember that in Chapters 2 and 3 we discussed the issues of offenders being "known" to authorities, and a lot of the time, this means that they were risk assessed but not prioritized. This does not mean that they did not look like they posed a risk but instead that *compared to all the other people* who were risk assessed, they seemed to all pose a similar risk and there were not enough resources to focus on everyone. So when it comes to the psychology of prevention, the main issue is identifying factors that are unique to those who are high risk but not those who are low risk, and, as you will remember from Chapter 2, this is very hard to do because terrorists are so often thought of as "demographically unremarkable" with no defining traits or qualities. Given the breadth of what it means to be "a terrorist," it is no surprise that there is an immense depth in the risk factors for being a terrorist. There are over 100 variables identified that could have implications for risk assessment (Gill et al., 2014). For example, in a recent review of risk factors for involvement in terrorism conducted by the National Institute of Justice (NIJ) through a conference examining risk assessment research and an examination of NIJ-funded research (Smith et al., 2016), the following factors were identified:

- Experiencing identity conflict/being a loner
- Feeling there is a lack of meaning in life
- Wanting status
- Failing to achieve aspirations
- Wanting to belong/trouble with platonic relationships
- Trouble in romantic relationships
- Desiring action or adventure/military experience
- Having experienced trauma/abuse
- Having mental health issues or being emotionally unstable/troubled
- Being naïve or having little knowledge of religion and ideology
- Stressors (e.g., a family crisis, being fired from a job)
- Having strong religious beliefs/extremist ideology
- Having grievances
- Feeling under threat
- Having an "us versus them" worldview

- Justifying violence or illegal activity as a solution to problems
- Having engaged in previous criminal activity
- Involvement with a gang or delinquent peers
- Societal discrimination or injustice
- Exposure to violent extremist groups or
- Exposure to violent extremist belief systems or narratives
- Family members or friends in a violent extremist network

As another (quick) activity, look at the list shown here and answer how many factors you exhibit. Better yet, in this chart, why not fill in the list for both you and Dylann Roof.

	You	DR
- Experiencing identity conflict/ being a loner	-	-
- Feeling there is a lack of meaning in life	-	-
- Wanting status	-	-
- Failing to achieve aspirations	-	-
- Wanting to belong/trouble with platonic relationships	-	-
- Trouble in romantic relationships	-	-
- Desiring action or adventure/ military experience	-	-
- Having experienced trauma/abuse	-	-
- Having mental health issues or being emotionally unstable/troubled	-	-
- Being naïve or having little knowledge of religion and ideology	-	-
- Stressors (e.g., a family crisis, being fired from a job)	-	-
- Having strong religious beliefs/ extremist ideology	-	-
- Having grievances	-	-
- Feeling under threat	-	-

	You	DR
- Having an "us versus them" worldview	-	-
- Justifying violence or illegal activity as a solution to problems	-	-
- Having engaged in previous criminal activity	-	-
- Involvement with a gang or delinquent peers	-	-
- Societal discrimination or injustice	-	-
- Exposure to violent extremist groups or individuals	-	-
- Exposure to violent extremist belief systems or narratives		
- Family members or friends in a violent extremist network		
Totals:		

What did you find? It may be that you are much closer to Dylann Roof than you would have expected (especially given the size of the risk difference between you, a reader of a book on terrorism, and Dylann Roof, a lone-actor terrorist). What I hope the reader has seen here is the full circle of terrorism, in that the questions that we are unable to answer at the start of the book directly feed into the questions we are unable to answer in later chapters, such as risk assessment and prevention. This is why understanding the psychology of the terrorist is so pervasive, because these fundamental questions of what separates "us" and "them" is the first step in being able to accurately and correctly prevent and counter future acts of terrorism.

CONCLUSIONS: PREVENTION TAKES A VILLAGE

We showed earlier that risk assessment is hard. It is a quest that psychologists are exploring and conducting some excellent work on, but because of the natural problem of terrorism (base rates and diversity), it will always be an uphill battle. So it is worth it to take a moment to highlight a few other opportunities for intervention that are both receiving significant attention and are relevant in the case of Dylann Roof. The first issue is increasing the role of peers and bystanders in intervening in instances where someone appears to be at risk. In Roof's case, there was a network of friends and family who could have intervened. In her article in GQ, Rachel Ghansah (2017) writes:

> One person who spent time in the trailer park with Roof agreed to talk with me on the condition that I didn't name them. When I asked what was most memorable about Roof, the answer came quickly: "He was quiet, uncomfortably quiet, strangely quiet. I mean really strange." But in this wasteland, with this group of listless friends, Roof could talk about shooting up a college, brandish his gun, use racist slurs, all without being considered outlandish. These instances evaporated into their ears as liquored-up loose talk. To this day, Roof's friends seem to have a striking inability to process the gravity of what he did. They have said things like: "He would talk about killing people, but none of us took him seriously."[5]

One of his friends also, for a period, took Roof's gun from him. There is also the gun itself. Since he had been arrested for drug use, Roof was not legally allowed to carry a gun. Finally, there is his online behavior. As he writes (noting I highlighted this quote earlier):

> The event that truly awakened me was the Trayvon Martin case. I kept hearing and seeing his name, and eventually I decided to look him up. I read the Wikipedia article and right away I was unable to understand what the big deal was. It was obvious that Zimmerman was in the right. But more importantly this prompted me to type in the words "black on White crime" into Google, and I have never been the same since that day.

It is the challenge of psychologists to work to understand the processes that are at play both in the terms of Roof's trajectory toward risk, as well as the barriers to intervening that may be experienced by his peers and family. Increasingly, both governments and psychologists are realizing that prevention is a full-scale effort that requires an understanding of the individual, their online interactions, and their community and peers, each of which provides critical points for intervention and, indeed, prevention.

6

CONCLUSION

REDUCTIONISM IN ART, SCIENCE, AND THE STUDY OF THE TERRORIST

Nobel Prize winner Eric R. Kandel recently wrote a book titled *Reductionism in Art and Brain Science* in which he argued that reductionism – the distillation of larger scientific or aesthetic concepts into smaller, more tractable components – has been used by scientists and artists alike to pursue their respective truths. Reductionism is the idea that all of the complex and apparently disparate things we observe in the world can be explained in terms of universal principles governing their common ultimate constituents (Nagel, 1998). In a scientific sense, it is incredibly appealing to believe that complex phenomena in our social and political world can be distilled down into simple, and indeed separate, phenomena; put simply, of causes and effects, or "terrorists" and "everyone else." The reality of the world is that it is far more complex, and underneath all of the simple processes that we think we see are the nuanced, complex processes that truly explain a phenomenon in the real world. It is then the challenge for scientists to not just understand the full complexity of the phenomena, but to be able to articulate that to the general public so that it can begin to see past the simple rules that it thinks govern behavior and appreciate the complexity of the problem at hand.

Perhaps because of the immense publicity that acts of terrorism, and the threat of terrorism, receive, it is especially prone to these simplistic rules. The basic assumptions of terrorism (who the terrorist is, how they behave, what motivates them) are repeated to us via film, television, and even in the media depictions of real terrorist attacks so that it almost creates a self-fulfilling prophecy, in which we report on the phenomenon in the way we expect it to manifest in the real world. But the truth is that terrorism is an immensely multifaceted and complex behavior. And, more unfortunately yet, it is one that is immensely hard to study. Consider this for a thought experiment. The following statement was written in the abstract of a 2019 paper on empathy (a core human emotion; see Zaki, 2019):

> When individuals experience empathy, they often seek to bolster others' well-being. But what do empathizers want others to feel? Though psychologists have studied empathy and prosociality for decades, this question has yet to be clearly addressed.

Empathy is a core human function; it is central to a range of important pro-social functions and is often viewed as a cornerstone of a good and healthy society. We can study empathy in the real world; there are millions of acts of empathy every day. We have all been, to varying degrees, empathetic, and we can observe empathy in others. In addition to this, we can *create* empathy in a laboratory. We can create paradigms where you have to experience true empathy, and we can manipulate different factors in the environment and see how this influences the amount of empathy that you may show. Thus, empathy is prevalent and visible, an experience we all have, and a phenomenon that can be exhibited and measured in a laboratory. And *still* after decades of research, central questions remain unanswered.

Now let us look at terrorism. There are not millions of acts of terrorism every day (in fact, globally, terrorism is decreasing); we have not all been (in many cases, to any degree) involved in terrorism, and we do not often get the chance to observe terrorism in others. We cannot *create* terrorism in a laboratory, and we cannot make paradigms that make individuals experience the psychological feeling of being involved in terrorism, nor can we manipulate the environment in a way that will increase or decrease the likelihood that someone will engage in terrorist behavior. In this sense, the study of terrorism is fundamentally at odds with what we would view the *classic* psychological method. Now this does not mean that psychology cannot aid in the study of terrorism; on the contrary, I hold it true that psychology is one of (if not the) most important domain of study to understand an individual's choice to engage in terrorism (although I will, of course, note I am biased). But what it does mean is that despite needing psychologists to help us understand this deeply damaging real-world phenomenon, we are unable to use many of the methods that have helped us identify, develop, and test theories in the wider psychological field. Furthermore, in many cases it was (perhaps incorrectly) assumed that even if we could use these theories, they would not be relevant because terrorism is such a *unique* form of behavior. It was in this vacuum, between the context of real-world phenomena and the context in which we traditionally test theories, that the application of psychology was perhaps twisted. Many commentators before me have noted that the psychology of terrorism, while popular, lacked rigor and evidence, and often we relied on assumptions or metaphors (e.g., "staircases") rather than integrated psychological processes with variables labeled and the directionality of effects and interactions between them studied. Progress in this area is being made, for example, with an increased focus on experimental methods and efforts to collect data from people who have engaged in terrorist behavior, and we are seeing psychological research that better reflects the psychological method we have relied on for decades. For example, in a recent *New York Times* piece, Hamid (2020) outlined his (and his colleagues; Pretus et al., 2018) work that was using Magnetic Resonance Imaging (MRI) scans of radicalized Islamists. While one commentator claimed that the study made them "break out in hives,"[1] this study is one of the first to really blend traditional psychological methods of data collection with a sample of violent extremists.

What this book has sought to show is that the psychology of terrorism cannot be reduced to simple, binary claims of "terrorists" and "non-terrorists," or "being a terrorist" or "not being a terrorist," or of "starting terrorism" and "stopping terrorism." The psychology of terrorism is a nuanced and complex field of study, and the key to success in understanding the psychology of terrorism is not to fold in the face of pressure to answer simple questions that are asked of us in the aftermath of an attack ("how do we profile a terrorist?"), but to embrace the complexity and begin to ask smarter questions about the specific nature of terrorism. So much progress has been made here over the past decade, and many of these examples have been provided over the course of this book. It is the difference between the statements (as shown by Corner and Gill) "terrorists are not mentally ill" and "lone actor terrorists are more likely to suffer from schizophrenia, autistic spectrum disorder, or a delusional disorder." One question is a broad-brush statement and views terrorists as one homogenous group. The other embraces the nuances of both the terrorist and the psychological disorder which we are speaking about.

The problem with this quest for complexity is that we (the population) love simplicity. In my other world of research, I study decision-making, and there is an innate human loathing of complexity and uncertainty. Our brains work to create simplicity. We adopt schemas, create mental models, and over-focus on single simplistic variable explanations because they create nice, easy, "If X then Y" rules that we understand. This is how we are taught, and this is how stories tell us the world works, and so with terrorism, like with everything, we yearn for simplistic answers. In this sense the attempt to teach the true psychology of terrorism goes against some deeply human tendencies because terrorism raises immense uncertainty (and hence a desire for simplicity), hence the answer of "it's complicated" is not the easiest answer to give (or hear). Perhaps this is why sometimes the simplistic (yet incorrect) answer is often the one that receives the most attention and is best remembered. People want to hear that they are all "psychopaths" or that "they were radicalized" because it creates a simple story that we can understand. But in the real world, this masking of complex psychological processes with simplistic, heuristic-laden metaphors and concepts prevents the complex discussions that are required to prevent future acts of terrorism.

THE FUTURE

So, when we look to the future of the psychology of terrorism, what do we want to see? To me it is simple: humanization. Humanistic psychology is a psychological perspective that emphasizes the study of the whole person. Humanistic psychologists look at human behavior not only through the eyes of the observer but also through the eyes of the person doing the behaving. Dr. Diane Blau (2013) explains the humanistic movement as such:

> Humanistic psychology is founded on the premise that each person is unique and to be accepted and respected for his or her individual qualities and characteristics. Each person is a blend of biology, past and current experiences, and diverse abilities and untapped resources to respond to life circumstances. Each individual attributes personal meaning to people and events that occur in his or her life and makes choices based on subjective perceptions to living. Each person has the capacity and opportunity for growth and change.

Some of the fundamental assumptions of humanistic psychology include:

- The experiences of the person (thinking, sensing, perceiving, feeling, remembering, and so on) are central to understanding their behavior.
- Behavior can only be understood through their subjective experience.
- An accurate understanding of human behavior cannot be achieved by studying animals.

- Free will exists, and we should focus on the role of personal responsibility for self-growth and fulfillment. Behavior cannot be determined.
- Self-actualization (the need for a person to reach maximum potential) is natural.
- People are inherently good and will experience growth if provided with suitable conditions, especially during childhood.

A humanistic perspective also encourages us to remember that terrorists are *humans*, the same as us. While humanistic psychology emphasizes the uniqueness of a person's experience as central to explaining their behavior, what is also true is that we all share the same explainers of human behavior and we can make far more progress in the psychology of terrorism by applying psychology *to* terrorism rather than developing a new psychology *of* terrorism. For all the unique theories of radicalization that are developed, we can learn just as much by looking at traditional theories of psychology. Consider the Newburgh four case presented in Chapter 4. Yes, we can look at this case through the lens of radicalization, but we can also look at the role of conformity to an authority figure who was giving instructions and orders. In doing so, suddenly the famous studies of Milgram and Asch, who showed that people are highly influenced by the behavior of those around us, can explain a wealth of the real-world cases of terrorism we have seen. Here we can see that traditional perspectives from psychology help us understand, perhaps, why four individuals who showed little to no interest in radical Islam found themselves in a position where they were laying IED explosives outside mosques in Newburgh, New York.

Overall, an embrace of this perspective would encourage us to hold that the movement toward terrorism is often out of the innate drive toward self-betterment and that it is the result of an individual decision to engage in something that they feel would allow them to reach maximum potential growth. This is precisely what the quest for significance outlines. But at the same time, by accepting this principle and focusing on the autonomy of the individual to *choose* terrorism, we realize that one of the keys to stopping terrorism is not to control their choice for them, but to provide them with more appealing options that they would want to choose instead. This supports the idea of a holistic approach to countering terrorism in which we focus on developing a pro-social society that encourages positive experiences and engaging in positive pro-social movements.

FURTHER READING

APA Podcast. *Speaking of psychology: Getting into a terrorist's mind.* www.apa.org/research/action/speaking-of-psychology/terrorist-mind

Atran, S. et al. (2017). *Challenges in researching terrorism in the field.* www.cmu.edu/epp/people/faculty/research/Fischhoff-Science%20Atran%202017.pdf

Bjørgo, T. (2016). *Counter-terrorism as crime prevention: A holistic approach.* https://dl1.cuni.cz/pluginfile.php/568786/mod_resource/content/0/bjrgo2015.pdf

Corner, E., & Gill, P. (2016). *Mental health disorders and the terrorist: A research note probing selection effects and disorder prevalence.* www.tandfonline.com/doi/full/10.1080/1057610X.2015.1120099

Hofmann, D., & Schmid, A. (2012). *Selected literature on (i) Radicalization and recruitment, (ii) De-radicalization and dis-engagement, and (iii) Counter-radicalization and countering violent extremism.* www.terrorismanalysts.com/pt/index.php/pot/article/view/235/html

Horgan, J. (2008a). *Deradicalization or disengagement? A process in need of clarity and a counterterrorism initiative in need of evaluation.* www.terrorismanalysts.com/pt/index.php/pot/article/viewFile/32/65

Horgan, J. (2008b). *From profiles to pathways and roots to routes: Perspectives from psychology on radicalization into terrorism.* http://citeseerx.ist.psu.edu/viewdoc/download?doi=10.1.1.526.9520&rep=rep1&type=pdf

Horgan, J., Altier, M. B., Shortland, N. D., & Taylor, M. (2016). Walking away: The disengagement and deradicalization of a right-wing violent extremist. *Behavioral Sciences of Terrorism and Political Aggression, 9*(2), 63–77. doi:10.1080/19434472.2016.1156722

Hunter, S., Shortland, N. D., Crayne, M., & Ligon, G. M. (2017). Recruitment and selection in violent extremist organizations: Viewing through an industrial and organizational psychology lens. *The American Psychologist, 72*(3), 242–254.

Knefel, J. (2013). *Everything you've been told about radicalization is wrong.* www.rollingstone.com/politics/politics-news/everything-youve-been-told-about-radicalization-is-wrong-80445/

Price, E. (2012). *Terrorism in history, monographs, edited volumes, non-conventional literature and prime articles (incl. pre-1968 publications): Compiled and selected by Eric Price.* www.terrorismanalysts.com/pt/index.php/pot/article/view/price-terrorism-in-history/html

Program on Extremism. (2018). *ISIS in America.* https://extremism.gwu.edu/sites/g/files/zaxdzs2191/f/downloads/ISIS%20in%20America%20-%20Full%20Report.pdf

Schmid, A. (2012). *The revised academic consensus definition of terrorism.* www.terrorismanalysts.com/pt/index.php/pot/article/view/schmid-terrorism-definition/html

Sinai, J. (2008). *How to define terrorism.* www.terrorismanalysts.com/pt/index.php/pot/article/view/33/html

Sinai, J. (2017). *Counterterrorism bookshelf: 30 books on terrorism & counter-terrorism-related subjects.* www.terrorismanalysts.com/pt/index.php/pot/article/view/644/html

NOTES

CHAPTER 1

1 Hat tip to Holbrook et al. (2013) for the use of this term in their work on identifying terroristic material on the Internet.
2 See van Zandt (2018) for more on this.
3 See Collins (2017) for a full outline of the public view of Jac Holmes.
4 See Welch (2013) for a full outline of the speech in which Christopher Dorner was labelled a "terrorist."
5 See Radil and Pinos (2019) for a good example of this.
6 https://www.thetimes.co.uk/article/transcript-of-woolwich-killer-speech-its-an-eye-for-an-eye-q35fzrmdz0k
7 See Silver, J., Horgan, J., & Gill, P. (2018). Foreshadowing targeted violence: Assessing leakage of intent by public mass murderers. *Aggression and Violent Behavior*, 38, 94–100.
8 Information about Jac Holmes' funeral is outlined in Blake (2017).

CHAPTER 2

1 Intelligence and Security Committee of Parliament [ISCP], 2014.
2 Joint Commonwealth NSW Review, 2015.
3 Hat tip to Paul Gill and Emily Corner for the *Lord of the Rings* quote.
4 They are of course not the first, or the only, psychologists to explore this, and much of their work integrates prior reviews of the field.

5 If this is sounding a little Freudian, that is not surprising. Narcissistic rage is a key theory of Sigmund Freud, and many of the early personality theories invoked psychoanalytical components (see Gill & Corner, 2017).

6 I acknowledge that I borrowed the inspiration for this analogy from Tyler Cote at Operation250 (www.operation250.org).

7 If there are any errors in the presentation of I/O psychology, I blame my mentor, Matthew Crayne.

8 Even if I do say so myself.

9 This also explains any typos that appear in this book.

10 This calculation was originally laid out in Horgan et al. (2018).

CHAPTER 3

1 Thomas Riegler does an excellent job of outlining the role of Hollywood in the modern depiction of terrorism in his 2010 paper "Through the Lenses of Hollywood: Depictions of Terrorism in American Movies."

2 Though it is worth noting that the view is that this was a threat and that at the crucial moment, he did not launch the missiles. Also, the movie is more enjoyable if you hold the belief that it is an unofficial Bond extension in which Sean Connery continues his role as James Bond.

3 See Ward (2007) for a discussion of this.

4 These theories are outlined in detail by King and Taylor (2011).

5 Group think is the psychological process in which a group all begins to think as one and becomes increasingly sure that their view is correct. They stop listening to alternate evidence and alternate approaches. They stop people from joining who do not agree. Group think, as a psychological process, is linked to risky decision-making, and some of the worst cases of decision errors in a range of contexts, even presidential decisions such as when to go to war.

6 United States Attorney's Office Southern District of New York (2010).

7 The source of these details can be found at United States Attorney's Office Southern District of New York (2011).

8 All of these details are outlined in Harris (2011).

9 See at United States Attorney's Office Southern District of New York (2013a, 2013b, 2013c).

10 FBI email dated April 1, 2009, in at United States Attorney's Office Southern District of New York (2013).

11 US Attorney's Office, Press Release, 2010a.

12 US Attorney's Office, Press Release, 2011.

13 See Slozdra (2013) for more information on this sting operation.

14 See Cabral (2010).

15 *United States of America vs. Cromitie et al.*, judicial opinion.

16 Ibid.

17 Ibid.

18 Ibid.

19 Ibid.

20 United States District Court Southern District of New York (2010). Decision and Order Regarding Bail and Speedy Trial. Retrieved from http://www.projectsalam.org/downloads/USA_v_Cromitie_decision.pdf

21 You may be noticing a family trend here, until I broke it and declared I wanted to be a psychologist.

CHAPTER 4

1 See BBC news report on the London Bridge perpetrator (Simone, 2019).

2 These are outlined elsewhere by Sabbagh (2020), although there is a wide range of concern around the use of lie detectors given that they are viewed as very inaccurate and currently inadmissible in court.

3 For example, Altier, Boyle, and Horgan (2020).

4 In this section, and indeed for the rest of the chapter, we focus only on instances where an individual chooses to leave terrorism behind, and not the process of voluntary or involuntary group disengagement, where a whole group disbands.

5 The reader is encouraged to visit the original for the full outline of the case; see Horgan et al. (2016).

6 The United Kingdom government reported that convicted terrorists will face lie-detector tests under a raft of measures drawn up in the wake of the London Bridge attack to toughen up the monitoring of offenders in the community (see Attwood, 2020).

7 This is one United Kingdom-based policy that was used on individuals who left the country to join ISIS.

CHAPTER 5

1 The full essay can be found in Ghansah (2017).

2 Crime scene details taken from sworn affidavits: www.scribd.com/doc/269162008/Dylann-Roof-affidavits

3 These excerpts are taken from a published version of the manifesto found here: https://talkingpointsmemo.com/muckraker/dylann-roof-manifesto-full-text

4 The nuances of these arguments are outlined in a recent article by Rhodan (2017).

5 https://www.tribes.org/web/2017/11/13/a-most-american-terrorist-the-making-of-dylann-roof

CHAPTER 6

1 This was a tweeted comment in response to the posting by a political scientist at Harvard University (https://twitter.com/jkertzer/status/1234495868155256832).

BIBLIOGRAPHY

Aho, J. A. (1988). Out of hate: A sociology of defection from neo-Nazism. *Current Research on Peace and Violence*, 11, 159–168.

Altier, M. B., Boyle, E., & Horgan, J. G. (2020). Terrorist transformations: The link between terrorist roles and terrorist disengagement, studies in conflict & terrorism. *Studies in Conflict and Terrorism*. doi: 10.1080/1057610

Altier, M. B., Boyle, E. L., Shortland, N. D., & Horgan, J. G. (2017). Why they leave: An analysis of terrorist disengagement events from eighty-seven autobiographical accounts. *Security Studies*, 26(2), 305–332.

Altier, M. B., Horgan, J., & Thoroughgood, C. (2013). In their own words? Methodological considerations in the analysis of terrorist autobiographies. *Journal of Strategic Studies*, 5(4), 85–98.

Altier, M. B., Thoroughgood, C., & Horgan, J. (2014). Turning away from terrorism: Lessons from psychology, criminology, and terrorism. *Journal of Peace Research*, 51(5), 647–661.

Attwood, M. (2020, January 21). Lie-detector tests for terrorist convicts are just a Hollywood stunt. *The Guardian*. www.theguardian.com/politics/2020/jan/21/lie-detector-tests-for-terrorist-convicts-are-just-a-hollywood-stunt

Bever, L. (2015, March 11). Dzhokhar Tsarnaev's scrawled message: "We Muslims are one body, you hurt one you hurt us all." *The Washington Post*. https://www.washingtonpost.com/news/morning-mix/wp/2015/03/11/dzhokhar-tsarnaevs-scrawled-message-we-muslims-are-one-body-you-hurt-one-you-hurt-us-all/

Bjørgo, T. (Ed.). (1997). *Racist and right-wing violence in Scandanavia.* Oslo: Tano-Aschehoug.

Bjørgo, T. (2009). Processes of disengagement from violent groups of the extreme right. In T. Bjøro & J. Horgan (Eds.), *Leaving terrorism behind: Individual and collective disengagement* (pp. 30–48). New York, NY: Routledge.

Bjørgo, T. (2011) Dreams and disillusionment: Engagement in and disengagement from militant extremist groups. *Crime, Law and Social Change,* 55(4), 277–285.

Bjørgo, T., & Horgan, J. (Eds.). (2009). *Leaving terrorism behind: Individual and collective disengagement.* London: Routledge.

Blake, M. (2017, February 2). Anti-Isis fighters gather in Dorset for funeral of UK sniper Jac Holmes. *The Guardian.* www.theguardian.com/uk-news/2018/feb/02/anti-isis-fighters-gather-in-dorset-for-funeral-of-uk-sniper-jac-holmes

Blau, D. (2013). Why humanistic psychology is a specialty to consider. *Michigan School of Psychology Blog Series.* https://msp.edu/why-humanistic-psychology-is-a-specialty-to-consider/

Borum, R. (2003, July). Understanding the terrorist mindset. *FBI Law Enforcement Bulletin,* 7–10.

Borum, R., Fein, R., Vossekuil, B., & Berglund, J. (1999). Threat assessment: Defining an approach for evaluating risk of targeted violence. *Behavioral Sciences & the Law,* 17(3), 323–337.

Cabral, L. R. (2010, November 12). Slide show: Were the Newburgh four victims of FBI entrapment? *The Nation.* www.thenation.com/article/archive/slide-show-were-newburgh-four-victims-fbi-entrapment/

Canter, D. (2000). Offender profiling and criminal differentiation. *Legal and Criminological Psychology,* 5(Part 1), 23–46.

Carraud, S. (2020, January 4). French knife attacker was radicalized, anti-terrorism prosecutors say. *Reuters.* https://www.reuters.com/article/us-france-security/french-knife-attacker-was-radicalized-anti-terrorism-prosecutors-say-idUSKBN1Z30JX

Chermak, S., & Gruenewald, J. A. (2015). Laying a foundation for the criminological examination of right-wing, left-wing, and Al Qaeda-inspired extremism in the United States. *Terrorism and Political Violence,* 27, 133–159. http://dx.doi.org/10.1080/09546553.2014.975646

Cole, J., Alison, E., Cole, B., & Alison, L. (2010). *Guidance for identifying people vulnerable to recruitment into violent extremism.* Liverpool: University of Liverpool, School of Psychology.

Collins, D. (2018). BRIT HERO TRAGEDY Brit volunteer fighter Jac Holmes killed by landmine in Syria just days after booting ISIS fanatics out of terror capital Raqqa. *The Sun.* www.thesun.co.uk/news/4753355/anti-isis-fighter-jac-holmes-killed-fighting-terror-group-alongside-kurds-in-syria/

Corner, E., Bouhana, N., & Gill, P. (2019). The multifinality of vulnerability indicators in lone-actor terrorism. *Psychology, Crime & Law, 25*(2), 111–132.

Dearden, L. (2019). Jihadi Jack: Parents of British Isis fighter spared jail for funding terrorism. *The Independent.* https://www.independent.co.uk/news/uk/crime/jihadi-jack-parents-trial-sally-lane-john-letts-syria-terror-funding-a8969141.html

Ebaugh, H. R. F. (1988). *Becoming an ex: The process of role exit.* Chicago: University of Chicago Press.

Freilich, J. D., & LaFree, G. (2015). Criminology theory and terrorism: Introduction to the special issue. *Terrorism and Political Violence, 27,* 1–8.

Ghansah, R. K. (2017). A most American terrorist: The making of Dylann Roof. *GQ.* https://www.gq.com/story/dylann-roof-making-of-an-american-terrorist

Gill, P., & Corner, E. (2013). Disaggregating terrorist offenders: Implications for research and practice. *Criminology & Public Policy, 12,* 93.

Gill, P., & Corner, E. (2017). There and back again: The study of mental disorder and terrorist involvement. *American Psychologist, 72*(3), 231–241.

Gill, P., Corner, E., Conway, M., Thornton, A., Bloom, M., & Horgan, J. (2017). Terrorist use of the internet by the numbers: Quantifying behaviors, patterns, and processes. *Criminology & Public Policy, 16*(1), 99–117.

Gill, P., & Horgan, J. (2013). Who were the volunteers? The shifting sociological and operational profile of 1240 provisional Irish Republican army members. *Terrorism and Political Violence, 25*(3), 435–456.

Gill, P., Horgan, J., & Deckert, P. (2014). Bombing alone: Tracing the motivations and antecedent behaviors of lone-actor terrorists. *Journal of Forensic Sciences, 59*(2), 425–435.

Gruenewald, J., Chermak, S., & Freilich, J. D. (2013a). Distinguishing "loner" attacks from other domestic extremist violence: A comparison of far-right homicide incident and offender characteristics. *Criminology & Public Policy, 12*(1), 65–91.

Gruenewald, J., Chermak, S., & Freilich, J. D. (2013b). Far-right lone wolf homicides in the United States. *Studies in Conflict & Terrorism, 36*(12), 1005–1024.

The Guardian. (2014). Lee Rigby murder: The judge's sentencing speech in full. https://www.theguardian.com/uk-news/2014/feb/26/lee-rigby-murder-judges-speech-sentencing

Gudjonsson, G. H. (2009). The assessment of terrorist offenders: A commentary on the Dernevik et al. article and suggestions for future directions. *The Journal of Forensic Psychiatry & Psychology*, 20(4), 516–519.

Gudjonsson, G. H., West, A., & McKee, A. (2015). Risk assessment of terrorist offenders: A challenge too far? In J. Pearse (Ed.), *Investigating terrorism: Current political, legal and psychological issues* (p. 123–143). Wiley-Blackwell.

Hamid, N. (2020, March 2). What I learned from scanning the brains of potential terrorists. *New York Times*. https://www.nytimes.com/2020/03/02/opinion/domestic-terrorism-jihadists.html

Handler, J. (1990). Socioeconomic profile of an American terrorist. *Terrorism*, 13, 195–213.

Harris, P. (Dec 12, 2011). Newburgh Four: Poor, black, and jailed under FBI 'entrapment' tactics. *The Guardian*. https://www.theguardian.com/world/2011/dec/12/newburgh-four-fbi-entrapment-terror

Holbrook, D., Ramsay, G., & Taylor, M. (2013). "Terroristic content": Towards a grading scale. *Terrorism and Political Violence*, 25, 2, 202–223.

Horgan, J. (2006). Disengaging from terrorism. *Jane's Intelligence Review*, 18(12), 34–37.

Horgan, J. (2008). From profiles to pathways and roots to routes: Perspectives from psychology on radicalization into terrorism. *The Annals of the American Academy of Political and Social Science*, 618, 80–94.

Horgan, J. (2009). *Walking away from terrorism: Accounts of disengagement from radical and extremist movements*. London: Routledge.

Horgan, J. (2011). Interviewing the terrorists: Reflections on fieldwork and implications for psychological research. *Behavioral Sciences of Terrorism and Political Aggression*, 4(3), 195–211.

Horgan, J. (2012). Interviewing the terrorists: Reflections on fieldwork and implications for psychological research. *Behavioral Sciences of Terrorism and Political Aggression*, 4(3), 195–211.

Horgan, J. (2014). *Psychology of terrorism* (2nd ed.). London: Routledge.

Horgan, J. (2019). Psychological approaches to the study of terrorism. In E. Chenoweth, R. English, A, Gofas, & S. Kalyvas (Eds). *The Oxford handbook of terrorism*. Oxford: Oxford University Press. DOI: 10.1093/oxfordhb/9780198732914.013.51

Horgan, J., & Altier, M. B. (2012). The future of terrorist de-radicalization programs. *Georgetown Journal of International Affairs*, Summer–Fall, 83–90.

Horgan, J., Altier, M. B., Shortland, N., & Taylor, M. (2012). Walking away: The
disengagement and de-radicalization of a violent right-wing extremist.
Behavioral Sciences of Terrorism and Political Aggression, 9(2), 63–77.

Horgan, J., & Braddock, K. (2010). Rehabilitating the terrorists? Challenges in
assessing the effectiveness of de-radicalization programs. *Terrorism and Polit-
icalViolence*, 22(1), 1–25.

Horgan, J., Shortland, N. D., & Abbasciano, S. (2018). Towards a typology of
terrorism involvement: A behavioral differentiation of violent extremist
offenders. *Journal of Threat Assessment and Management*, 5(2), 84–102.

Horgan, J., Shortland, N., Abbasciano, S., & Walsh, S. (2016). Actions speak
louder than words: A behavioral analysis of 183 individuals convicted for
terrorist offenses in the United States from 1995 to 2012. *Journal of Forensic
Sciences*, 61(5), 1228–1237.

Horgan, J., & Taylor, M. (2011). Disengagement, de-radicalization and the arc
of terrorism: Future directions for research. In R. Coolsaet (Ed.), *Jihadi
terrorism and the radicalization challenge: European and American experiences* (2nd ed.,
pp. 173–186). London: Ashgate.

Hussain, M. (2020, January 21). A new book takes on the problem of "jihadism."
The Intercept. https://theintercept.com/2020/01/21/jihadism-universal-
enemy-book-darryl-li/

Kebbell, M. R., & Porter, L. (2012). An intelligence assessment framework for
identifying individuals at risk of committing acts of violent extremism
against the West. *Security Journal*, 25(3), 212–228.

King, M., & Taylor, D. M. (2011). The Radicalization of Homegrown Jihadists: A
Review of Theoretical Models and Social Psychological Evidence. *Terrorism
and Political Violence*, 23(4), 602–622.

Kinsley, M. (2001). Defining terrorism. *The Washington Post*. https://owl.purdue.
edu/owl/research_and_citation/apa_style/apa_formatting_and_style_
guide/reference_list_electronic_sources.html

Knefel, J. (2013, May 6). Everything you've been told about radicalization is
wrong. *Rolling Stone*. https://www.rollingstone.com/politics/politics-news/
everything-youve-been-told-about-radicalization-is-wrong-80445/

Kruglanski, A. W., Gelfand, M. J., Bélanger, J. J., Gunaratna, R., & Hettiarachchi, M.
(2014). De-radicalising the liberation tigers of tamil eelam (LTTE): Some

preliminary findings. In A. Silke (Ed). *Prisons, Terrorism and Extremism: Critical Issues in Management, Radicalisation and Reform* (pp. 183–196). Taylor and Francis. https://doi.org/10.4324/9780203584323

Lemieux, P. (2014). Grudge, vengeance boredom. https://www.econlib.org/grudge-vengeance-and-boredom/

Lemieux, P. (Aug 5, 2018). "Grudge, Vengence, and Boredom." *The Library of Economics and Liberty.* https://www.econlib.org/grudge-vengeance-and-boredom/

Levenson, E., & Burnside, T. (2020, January 29). Dylann Roof believed he'd be freed from prison after a race war, attorneys say in appeal. CNN. https://www.cnn.com/2020/01/29/us/dylann-roof-appeal/index.html

McCauley, C., & Moskalenko, S. (2008). Mechanisms of political radicalization: Pathways toward terrorism. *Terrorism and Political Violence, 20*(3), 415–433.

McCauley, C., & Moskalenko, S. (2011). *Friction: How radicalization happens to them and us.* Oxford: Oxford University Press.

McCauley, C., & Moskalenko, S. (2017). Understanding political radicalization: The two-pyramids model. *American Psychologist, 72*(3), 205–216.

Meloy, J. R. (2011, July). Violent true believers. *FBI Law Enforcement Bulletin,* 24–32.

Meloy, J. R., & Genzman, J. (2016). The clinical threat assessment of the lone-actor terrorist. *Psychiatric Clinics, 39*(4), 649–662.

Meloy, J. R., & Gill, P. (2016). The lone-actor terrorist and the TRAP-18. *Journal of Threat Assessment and Management, 3*(1), 37.

Meloy, J. R., Hoffmann, J., Guldimann, A., & James, D. (2012). The role of warning behaviors in threat assessment: An exploration and suggested typology. *Behavioral Sciences & the Law, 30*(3), 256–279.

Meloy, J. R., & Yakeley, J. (2014). The violent true believer as a "lone wolf" – Psychoanalytic perspectives on terrorism. *Behavioral Sciences & the Law, 32*(3), 347–365.

Merari, A. (2010). *Driven to death: Psychological and social aspects of suicide terrorism.* Oxford: Oxford University Press.

Moghaddam, F. M. (2005). The staircase to terrorism: A psychological exploration. *American Psychologist, 60,* 161–169. http://dx.doi.org/10.1037/0003-066X.60.2.161

Monahan, J. F. (2011). *Numerical methods of statistics.* Cambridge: Cambridge University Press.

Monahan, J. F. (2012). The individual risk assessment of terrorism. *Psychology, Public Policy, and Law, 18*(2), 167.

Monahan, J. F. (2017). The individual risk assessment of terrorism: Recent developments. *The Handbook of the Criminology of Terrorism*, 520–534.

Nagel, T. (1998). Reductionism and antireductionism. In G. R. Bock and J. A. Goode (Eds.), *The limits of reductionism in biology* (pp. 3–10). Chichester: John Wiley & Sons.

Newcombe, Peter A., & Boyle, Gregory J. (1995). High school students' sports personalities: Variations across participation level, gender, type of sport, and success. *International Journal of Sport Psychology*, 26, 277–294.

O'Shea, D. S., & Yan, H. (2016, December 14). Dylann Roof's racist rants read in court. CNN. https://www.cnn.com/2016/12/13/us/dylann-roof-murder-trial/index.html

Pearlstein, R. M. (1991). *The mind of the political terrorist*. Wilmington, DE: Scholarly Resources Inc.

Pretus, C., Hamid, N., Sheikh, H., Ginges, J., Tobeña, A., et al. (2018). Neural and behavioral correlates of sacred values and vulnerability to violent extremism. *Frontiers in Psychology*, 9, 2462.

Radil, S. M., & Pinos, J. C. (2019). Reexamining the four waves of modern terrorism: A territorial interpretation. *Studies in Conflict and Terrorism*. doi:10.1080/1057610

Rhodan, M. (2017, December 15). Dylann Roof found guilty of all charges in Charleston Church shooting. *TIME Magazine*. https://time.com/4603863/dylann-roof-verdict-guilty/

Riegler, T. (2010). Through the lenses of hollywood: Depictions of terrorism in American movies. *Perspectives on Terrorism*, 4(2), 22.

Roberts, K., & Horgan, J. (2008). Risk assessment and the terrorist. *Perspectives on Terrorism*, 2(6), 3–9.

Rodger, E. (2014). The manifesto of Elliott Rodger. *The New York Times*. https://www.nytimes.com/interactive/2014/05/25/us/shooting-document.html

Rose, L. (2018, May). US has 1,000 open ISIS investigations but a steep drop in prosecutions. *CNN*. https://www.cnn.com/2018/05/16/politics/isis-us-arrests-investigations-terrorism/index.html.

Sabbagh, D. (2020, January 22). Government terror adviser warns 'no magic test' to stop reoffending. *The Guardian*. www.theguardian.com/uk-news/2020/jan/22/government-terror-adviser-jonathan-hall-qc-criticises-lie-detector-plans

Sarma, K. M. (2017). Risk assessment and the prevention of radicalization from nonviolence into terrorism. *American Psychologist*, 72(3), 278.

Schuurman, B. (2018). Research on terrorism, 2007–2016: A review of data, methods, and authorship. *Terrorism and Political Violence*, 1–16.

Seierstad, A. (2013). *One of us: The story of Anders Breivik and the massacre in Norway*. New York: Farrar, Straus & Girouz.

Shebab, K. (2016). Muslim convert Jack Letts calls on Brits to turn to Islam. *The Independent*. https://web.archive.org/web/20180211084937/https://www.independent.co.uk/news/muslim-convert-jack-letts-calls-on-brits-to-turn-to-islam

Silver, J., Horgan, J., & Gill, P. (2018). Foreshadowing targeted violence: Assessing leakage of intent by public mass murderers. *Aggression and Violent Behavior, 38*, 94–100.

Simi, P., & Futrell, R. (2006). Cyberculture and the endurance of white power activism. *Journal of Political and Military Sociology, 34*, 115–142.

Simone, D. (2019, December 5). London Bridge: Who was the attacker? BBC News. https://www.bbc.com/news/uk-50611788

Slozdra, P. (2013, March 11). The FBI goes to disturbing lengths to set up potential terrorists. *Business Insider*. www.businessinsider.com/the-fbi-hatched-some-crazy-terror-plots-2013-3

Smith, B. (1994). *Terrorism in America: Pipe bombs and pipe dreams*. Albany: State University of New York Press.

Smith, B. L., Snow, D. A., Fitzpatrick, K., Damphousse, K. R., Roberts, P., Tan, A., Brooks, A., & Klein, K. (2016). *Identity and framing theory, precursor activity, and the radicalization process*. https://www.ncjrs.gov/pdffiles1/nij/grants/249673.pdf

Stern, J. (2014). X: A case study of a Swedish neo-Nazi and his reintegration into Swedish society. *Behavioral Sciences and the Law, 32*(3), 440–453.

Taylor, M. (1988). *The terrorist*. London: Brassey's.

Taylor, M. (1991). *The Fanatics: A Behavioural Approach to Political Violence*. London: Brassey's.

Taylor, M., & Horgan, J. (2006). A conceptual framework for addressing psychological process in the development of the terrorist. *Terrorism and Political Violence, 18*(4), 585–601.

Terrorist Trial Report Card. (2011). *September 11, 2001 – September 11, 2011*. New York: The Center on Law and Security, New York University of Law.

United States Attorney's Office Southern District of New York. (2010, October 18). Four men found guilty of plotting to bomb New York synagogue and Jewish community center and to shoot military planes with stinger missiles. Press Release. https://www.fbi.gov/newyork/press-releases/2010/nyfo101810.htm

United States Attorney's Office Southern District of New York. (2010a, October 18). Press Release, Four men found guilty of plotting to bomb New York synagogue and Jewish community center and to shoot military planes with stinger missiles. Retrieved from https://www.fbi.gov/newyork/press-releases/2010/nyfo101810.htm

United States Attorney's Office Southern District of New York. (2011, June 29). Three men each sentenced in Manhattan federal court to 25 years in prison for plotting to bomb Bronx synagogues and shoot down U.S. military planes. Press Release. https://www.fbi.gov/newyork/press-releases/2011/three-men-each-sentenced-in-manhattan-federal-court-to-25-years-in-prison-for-plotting-to-bomb-bronx-synagogues-and-shoot-down-u.s.-military-planes

United States Attorney's Office Southern District of New York. (2011, June 29). Press Release, Three men each sentenced in Manhattan federal court to 25 years in prison for plotting to bomb Bronx synagogues and shoot down U.S. military planes. Retrieved from https://www.fbi.gov/newyork/press-releases/2011/three-men-each-sentenced-in-manhattan-federal-court-to-25-years-in-prison-for-plotting-to-bomb-bronx-synagogues-and-shoot-down-u.s.-military-planes

United States District Court, S. D. New York. (2009, May 9). *United States of America vs., James Cromitie, David Williams, Onta Williams and Laguerre Payen, defendants, criminal complaint.* http://www.investigativeproject.org/documents/case_docs/990.pdf

United States District Court, S. D. New York. (2013a, August 22). *United States of America vs., James Cromitie, David Williams, Onta Williams and Laguerre Payen, defendants, judicial opinion.* http://caselaw.findlaw.com/us-2nd-circuit/1642475.html

United States District Court, S. D. New York. (2013b). *United States of America vs., James Cromitie, David Williams, Onta Williams and Laguerre Payen, transcripts* (Admitted 08-30-10). http://www.investigativeproject.org/documents/case_docs/1433.pdf

United States District Court, S. D. New York. (2013c). *United States of America vs., James Cromitie, David Williams, Onta Williams and Laguerre Payen, transcripts* (Admitted 08-31-10). http://www.investigativeproject.org/documents/case_docs/1434.pdf

Van Zandt, C. (2018). What makes a serial bomber click. *The Atlantic.* www.theatlantic.com/health/archive/2018/03/what-makes-a-serial-bomber-tick/556922/

Ward, L. (2007, January 7). From Aladdin to Lost Ark, Muslims get angry at "bad guy" film images: Crude and exaggerated stereotypes are fuelling Islamophobia, says study. *The Guardian.* www.theguardian.com/media/2007/jan/25/broadcasting.race

Webster, W. H., Winter, D. E., Adrian, L., Steel, J., Baker, W. M., Bruemmer, R. J., & Wainstein, K. L. (2012). *Final report of the William H. Webster Commission on the Federal Bureau of Investigation, counterterrorism intelligence, and the events at Fort Hood, Texas on November 5, 2009.* Technical report, Federal Bureau of Investigation.

Welch, M. W. (2013, February 10). LAPD: Fugitive ex-cop a "domestic terrorist." *USA Today.* www.usatoday.com/story/news/nation/2013/02/10/ex-cop-manhunt-continues/1906999/

Wolf, M., Van Doorn, G. S., Leimar, O., & Weissing, F. J. (2007). Life-history trade-offs favour the evolution of animal personalities. *Nature, 447*(7144), 581.

Youngs, D. (2006). How does crime pay? The differentiation of criminal specialisms by fundamental incentive. *Journal of Investigative Psychology and Offender Profiling, 3,* 1–19.

Zaki, J. (2019). Integrating empathy and interpersonal emotion regulation. *Annual Review of Psychology, 71,* 517–540.